BEYOND
NOMINATING

BEYOND NOMINATING

A Guide To Gaining and Sustaining Successful Not-For-Profit Boards. *by* George B. Wright

C3 Publications
Portland, Oregon

BEYOND NOMINATING

A Guide to Gaining and Sustaining
Successful Not-For-Profit Boards

Published by C3 Publications
A Division of C3 Strategies
3495 NW Thurman Street
Portland, Oregon 97210

First Edition

Library of Congress Catalogue Card Number 96-085840
ISBN 0-9632655-1-2

Book design by: Merritt & Riley Visual Communications

Cover and theme design by: Dan Fast Creative

Printed in the United States of America

For Betsy
for always believing

"Instead of trying to recruit volunteers by promising them that it will make them feel better, non-profits should show people that in the process of taking care of others, they will grow. Through the act of giving, my whole self-concept is enlarged. I'm literally a stronger, more effective person."

—*Robert Wuthnow*

Preface

THIS ~~SHOULD~~ **WILL** BE FUN

Attracting the volunteer leadership needed to sustain board competency can be a daunting, I-hope-they-don't-ask-me-to-do-it task—if attempted without strategic direction. On the other hand, it can be an exhilarating challenge and great fun if those responsible work from realistic goals and stick to a plan of action. We definitely want you to enjoy this process!

Before you get under way, let's take a moment to consider your task.
Two assignments are involved:

1. replacing volunteer skills and experience as they cycle off of the board, and

2. adding new skills and experience not represented on the board, and at the same time improving board capability.

First, remember, board members do leave—it's as simple as that. Their terms expire. They move out of town. They take on new volunteer challenges. They burn out. Their life priorities change. This cycle is a fact of organizational life. So, one clear task is board member "succession planning," replacing your board's base of skill, access and experience. Making the people-moving transition as seamless as possible is a goal of board development.

However, an equally important challenge is to "expand" your board's capability to address the future needs of the organization. It is very unlikely that the board guiding your organization today will fit your needs five years from now. Status quo is not an option, especially when facing an accelerated pace of change, growing competition and your own future vision and goals.

Any organization, no matter how competent, can lose momentum, often for years, if it doesn't continually renew its board through pro-active recruitment. Obviously, an effective not-for-profit board requires a full complement of members with energy, knowledge and commitment. Committing to sound board development tactics will assure that your organization will be able to attract the leadership you want and need. And by sustaining board development, your organization need not suffer "feast or famine" leadership cycles.

A "side bar" to a board member's tenure is to, from time-to-time, ask: "Who is going to fill my shoes when I leave this board?" Is the process in place to assure that leadership won't falter in your absence? So maybe you aren't irreplaceable. It's the "replaceable" part that needs to be addressed. Part of your legacy to the organization is your successor.

Congratulations on your decision to sustain and enhance your board's capability.

Have fun!

Acknowledgments

My commitment to board development has always been enhanced by others who also have a passion for volunteer leadership. In the case of this manual, I want to extend my appreciation to the American Red Cross-Santa Clara Valley Chapter in San Jose, California, for serving as the test site for *Beyond Nominating*. A special thanks to Scott Render, Executive Director of the Santa Clara Valley Chapter, for allowing me to apply the concepts and methods of the book as part of our counsel to them on board development.

Naturally, we didn't start out with a complete process. We did, in fact, conduct a field test, modifying along the way as we worked with Scott's very able Board Development Committee. Whenever we ran into an "Aha!", I would hustle back to my computer and create a new step to address that specific need—then we would test it. We enjoyed ourselves, and Scott and his volunteers were successful. They committed to a process and stayed with it. The results were self-evident.

I also extend heartfelt thanks to Ron Gibbs, who helped me recognize the need for some major changes in the manual, while pointing out those pesky small details, and giving me much support and encouragement. Ron is Executive Director of the Woodland Park Zoological Society and teaches marketing for nonprofit organizations at the University of Washington in Seattle.

And a big thank you to Patti LaFore, my able right hand at C3 Publications; my sounding board and the best proofreader I've ever known.

Of course, the biggest support of all came from Betsy Wright, my life partner and professional partner as well. Together we share the challenge of serving our consulting clients' needs at C3 Strategies. She has also given me her unwavering support and input as I poured several years, many months and hours, into presenting my passion for the volunteer board in this book.

George B. Wright
Portland, Oregon

Contents

Section 1 GETTING READY TO GET READY

Section 2 GAME PLAN STRATEGIES

Section 3 RECRUITMENT A-C-T-I-O-N!

Section 4 FROM "HELLO" TO "GOOD-BYE"

Appendix

List of Worksheets, Forms & Guidelines

This table lists the various forms and guidelines, presented in each section, which can be used to implement the narrative steps.

Quotation References

William Conrad,	*The Effective Voluntary Board of Directors.* Swallow Press, 1983.
Robert D. Herman,	*Executive Leadership in Nonprofit Organizations.* Jossey–Bass, 1991.
Judith R. Saidel,	*Governing, Leading & Managing Nonprofit Organizations.* Jossey–Bass, 1993.
Thomas Wolf,	*The Nonprofit Organization.* Prentice–Hall, 1984.
Robert Wuthnow,	*Acts of Compassion: Caring for Others & Helping Ourselves.* Princeton's Center for the Study of American Religion, 1991.

Introduction

The primary challenge before all not-for-profit organizations is not about having a dramatic mission. There are many of those. Nor is it necessarily about raising the most dollars; though certainly financial resources are essential. The most significant challenge is to attract and sustain competent, visionary leadership at the board level. In effect, to go "beyond nominating" in seeking board leadership that is *limitless* in its vision and in its ability to assume the challenge of mission.

A Limitless Board . . .

- Is always capable of reaching organizational goals, while seeing a greater vision and sustaining its own capacity.

- Is made up of people who see their responsibilities clearly and accept them as a charge they willingly take up; who have not let themselves be coerced into reluctant service.

- Was created with thought, planning and attention to the current and future needs of the organization, with which a select few have been entrusted.

- Is a group of people who understand that, for the moment, they are the keepers of an organization's mission, and they strive to move it forward on their watch.

- Understands that leadership must be sustained, that it cannot be a "some time" thing, ebbing and flowing. There are no gaps.

- Understands that their term of service is temporary and that they must plan to sustain the quality of board leadership.

- Understands that for an organization of volunteers to excel, they will seek successors whose skills, experience and vision will match, or even exceed, that which they were able to give.

- Carries high the baton of service and is ready and prepared to pass it on without a stutter as their leg of the race comes full circle.

The *limitless* board is built with care and a view to the future. It draws upon its strength to meet the immediate needs of service, while building new strength among its numbers for the challenges and opportunities of the future. The limitless board never allows itself an "off season," or a "building year". The commitment is to sustain board competency, never yielding to apathy, or mediocrity.

As you prepare to enhance the capability of your organization's board, remember, it is never about filling vacant seats. It is about maintaining volunteer leadership that never falters. Most of all, it is about attracting people who see only possibilities, have a future vision and understand sustaining the mission. To get those people—you must go *beyond the act of nominating*.

How To Use This Book

Beyond Nominating is designed to help your organization manage the process of gaining and sustaining board leadership. Look at this book as a resource, a tool, for your Board Development or Nominating Committee, and Chief Executive. The book may serve as a guide from start to finish, or as a template, from which you pull out the necessary elements to facilitate your board building plans.

DECIDING WHERE YOU ARE IN THE PROCESS

First, I suggest getting a feel for the book. Scan the contents; the full scope and sequence. After reviewing the book, consider just where you are in your board development process. If you have completed some of the steps, evaluate your results; you may not need to re-do those tasks.

AVOIDING A PIECEMEAL APPROACH

Being as thorough as possible is important. Avoid the temptation to by-pass steps because you feel, "we don't need to do that." The biggest pitfall to board development success is avoiding process; side-stepping the planning infrastructure.

WHERE DO YOU BEGIN?

Where you start is up to you. If your board development has largely focused on a nominating exercise, or has been catch-as-catch-can, you will want to consider wiping the slate clean and begin with section one. If you feel that you have a good process but need help in specific areas, pick various steps, exercises or tools from the book to enhance what is already working.

HOW THE BOOK CAN HELP YOU

The book is designed in four sections:

1. *Getting Ready to Get Ready*

2. *Game Plan Strategies*

3. *Recruitment A-c-t-i-o-n*

4. *From "Hello" to "Good-Bye"*

These are the infrastructure of the process. Examine each section and consider the implications. Even if you think you have it covered, re-examination is often a worthwhile exercise. Each section begins with an explanatory narrative, several with *case-in-point* "vignettes," helping to set the stage for the process—pointing the way. Backing up each of the narratives are the tools to help move the process along. Use these tools as presented, or modify them to fit your needs. Other resources will be found in the Appendix. You acquired this book because your organization is committed to attracting the best volunteer leadership possible. Creating and sustaining a competent, visionary board takes commitment; commitment to mission, to quality and to process. Don't cut corners. Stay the course. Follow through. Have fun!

The Flow & Go

THE PROCESS

To reach your intended outcome, it is important to "stay on track." This means: *the process, the process, the process.* Every temptation to jump the gun, and cut out a step or two, should be considered carefully. The following is one example of a board development flow line. We are basing this graph on annual goals, set out in 90 day segments:

THE SEQUENCE

* Board Development Committee

THE WORKING DAYS SCHEDULE

Board Commits To Board Development Priority ▬▬ Day 1
Board Development Committee Is Appointed ▬▬▬▬ Day 15
BDC / Staff Complete Audit Of Board Status ▬▬▬▬▬ Day 25
BDC / Staff Complete Assessment Of Readiness ▬▬▬▬▬▬ Day 35
BDC Completes Board Development Plan ▬▬▬▬▬▬▬ Day 45
BDC Identifies / Qualifies Potential Candidates ▬▬▬▬▬▬▬ Day 55
Recruitment, Close And Election Of Candidates ▬▬▬▬▬▬▬▬▬ Day 80
Induction And Orientation Of New Members ▬▬▬▬▬▬▬▬▬▬ Day 90

THIS GRAPH USES A 90 DAY SCHEDULE

Strategically, you will be more successful in reaching your overall goals by breaking the process down into manageable time components. Annual goals can be achieved in short-term "bites," each to be achieved within 90 days. Volunteers will be able to see the "beginning" and the "end" of a project—and enjoy the success of their efforts. After a short-term goal has been achieved, your committee and staff can assess what worked and what needs changing—then set out to complete the next phase of your Board Development Plan. Through this continued effort, the organization receives a steady infusion of needed new talent, assuring a capable, "limitless" board.

GETTING READY TO GET READY

"If boards are more ceremonial than substantive, they are not acting as instruments of democracy and vehicles for meaningful citizen participation in community organizations."

—*Judith R. Saidel*

It Starts Here

....

The Commitment
Of The Board

THE COMPETITIVE EDGE FOR ATTRACTING
VOLUNTEER LEADERSHIP IS: *THE "ASK"*

Look at any successful not-for-profit organization and you will usually find a strong, competent and committed board of directors. A board which knows what is expected. A board which has been given the tools to do the job and is responding to the challenge. Such boards do not evolve simply because a mission is compelling. And they certainly don't come into being just because they were asked to serve. There is plenty of asking going on. It is the quality of the "ask," what went into the "ask" and what is backing up the "ask" that counts.

The best talent will be recruited heavily because they can lead an organization toward a dynamic new vision. In fact, they may also help design that new future and leverage the organization toward it with gusto! Such talent may very well go to another organization if your are not ready to commit to a quality effort of board development.

Commitment starts with the board, but is implemented by a capable Board Development Committee. This committee, which is charged with sustaining high quality volunteer leadership, ought to include members who are among the most experienced, most influential and most visionary volunteers available.

BOARD COMMITMENT: *ON THE RECORD*

Before engaging in board development or recruitment activities, commitment to board competence should be confirmed. It will send a positive signal if the board *goes on record,* confirming its commitment to the entire organization.

A model instrument, such as the one represented in Figure 1.1, can be used to ratify your board's commitment to sustaining competent leadership. The act of ratification can also serve as an opportunity to review board development and the board's role in the process. Once approved, the ratification document is signed by the Board President and Chief Executive, then kept with the official board minutes of that meeting.

Commitment to
Board Competence *Ratification*

BOARD RESOLUTION:

Understanding that capable and competent leadership is essential to the ongoing success of our organization, the board of directors of _____ hereby commits, on the date inscribed below, its full support to an ongoing board development strategy. With this commitment, the board recognizes the value and necessity for excellence in succession planning, recruitment, orientation and training of the current and future boards which will lead this organization.

FURTHER:

The board agrees to stand behind its commitment to board competence, offering to fully support and participate with the committee/committees charged to sustain the organization's board development strategies.

Organization: _____

Board President/Chair: _____

Executive Director/CEO: _____

Date of Ratification: _____

Note: The original copy of this signed document will be filed with the official board minutes of the date of ratification. Copies will be provided to the Board Development Committee.

FIGURE 1.1 ©*1996 C3 Publications*

Selecting a "Champion" and Forming the Committee

Steps To Creating The Team

Starting with the chairperson, the group of people who will orchestrate and drive the board development process should be enthusiastic about their task. Not only will they possess experience and knowledge, they will have insights about the future vision of the organization. The Board President should give careful consideration to the person, he/she selects to lead the Board Development Committee. That person will literally be a "champion," an evangelist, selling the committee's charge with conviction.

STANDING COMMITTEE

The board confirms the Board Development Committee as a standing committee, so reflected in the bylaws, complete with committee charge. See Figure 1.3. for Model Committee Charge. *(Note: Because nominating is but one step in the process, the title Board Development Committee is used here; however, use the committee name with which your organization is most comfortable.)*

CHAIR SELECTION

The Board President and Chief Executive work together to select the most capable leader available to lead the Board Development Committee. They confer with that person on selecting the other members. The chair will drive the process, so pick the best—pick a champion! See Figure 1.2 for Model Chair Job Description.

COMMITTEE SELECTION

The Committee Chair should spare no effort to form the best committee possible. And don't rush the process. If you must wait a short while to form the best team—do so. Perseverance in this quest will pay substantial dividends. Persons to consider for your Board Development Committee may include: past Board President/s, President-Elect, other officers, veteran board members who have solid organizational knowledge, and persons with access to minority representation, the business community, niche areas of specific interest to your organization, and overall vision of community culture. Consider committee members from outside the organization to add balance and zest to the process and help prevent the "cloning" exercise. See Figure 1.3 for Model Committee Charge.

M O D E L   D O C U M E N T

Chairperson Job Description
Board Development Committee

The Chair of the Board Development Committee will function best when his/her duties are clearly defined and supported by the Board and Board President. A specific and concise job description will confirm duties and responsibilities.

FUNCTION

- The Chairperson shall be responsible for guiding the work of the Committee and for facilitating the Committee's charge from the Board of Directors to sustain and grow board competency. The Chairperson shall assure the Board that the duties and time lines of the Committee are fulfilled and met as prescribed.

ACCOUNTABILITY

- The Chairperson is appointed by the Board President and accountable to the President and the Board of Directors.

RESPONSIBILITIES

- In accordance with the Board Development Committee Charge, appoint Committee members at least one month prior to the beginning of the organization's fiscal year.

- Facilitate the Committee in creating an annual plan for board development.

- Work with the Chief Executive Officer, seeking his/her input as part of an ongoing board development process.

- Maintain an active committee schedule and report regularly to the Board with progress reports, i.e., recommendations for board nominees, status of annual election of officers and overall interpretation of current and future board leadership goals.

QUALIFICATIONS

- Knowledge of, and experience in, organizational governance.

- Thorough understanding of organization's mission, programs and services, and future expectations, and a commitment to same.

- Demonstrated leadership experience and a sincere interest in developing the leadership competency of the organization and a willingness to commit time and energy to the Committee's charge.

- Meets guidelines for Board qualifications and the qualities and skills which are described in the Board of Directors Job Description.

FIGURE 1.2 ©1996 C3 Publications

MODEL DOCUMENT

Committee Charge from Board
Board Development Committee

As with the Chairperson, Committee members will get off to a quicker start, and be able to stay on track if they have been given clear guidance about the Committee's status, accountability and charge.

STANDING & ACCOUNTABILITY

■ The Board Development Committee (BDC) shall be a standing committee of the Board of Directors and so reflected in the organization's bylaws.

■ The Committee shall be chaired by (the President-Elect, Vice President, or other Board member; stipulate) appointed by the Board President.

■ The Committee Chair shall have the authority to appoint all members of the committee.

COMPOSITION & TERM OF SERVICE

■ The Committee shall be comprised of at least _____ members of the Board. The Committee Chair shall have the option of adding other Committee members from among other volunteers within the organization and/or qualified members at large from the community to provide the complement of experience, skills and knowledge required.

■ The Committee term for the Chair and members shall be for one year. Members may be appointed to additional years.

DUTIES

■ The Board Development Committee shall have the following duties:

— At the first meeting of the Board of Directors in each organizational year, the BDC shall present for recertification, the organization's formal statement of "Commitment to Board Competence" to be ratified by the board.

— The BDC shall audit the current board elective process, assess organizational readiness for its development duties, and create an annual board development plan. Also, by process, the BDC shall submit nominees for Board service in keeping with determined strategies, and attend to the indoctrination of new directors.

FIGURE 1.3 ©*1996 C3 Publications*

5

— The BDC shall have the duty of setting the slate of nominees for the officer positions of the Board to be submitted formally at the organization's annual meeting which is held in (month) of each year. *

— The BDC shall work in partnership with the Chief Executive Officer and look to him/her for guidance in establishing leadership needs and in meeting organization time lines for researching, recruiting and nominating duties.

— In all of its duties, the BDC shall keep the Board President and the Board informed of its progress and shall provide adequate notice, as prescribed by the bylaws, for all nominations and designated dates of appointment and/or election to the Board of Directors or officer positions.

— The BDC shall function on a year-round basis and shall submit nominees for Board Directorship as often as may be required to sustain a full complement of skills and experience to maintain board competence.

* Role of selecting the slate of officers, while an important duty of the Board Development or Nominating Committee, is beyond the scope of this book.

FIGURE 1.3 ©1996 C3 Publications

The Audit

....

Certifying how you
form your board

CASE IN POINT ⇨

Henry invited Chuck for lunch, on the vague premise of "something to discuss." After enduring small talk over fish and chips, Chuck squinted over a cup of coffee. "Okay, Henry, what's up?"

Henry cleared his throat. "Well, it's like this. I'm on the nominating committee for the Arts Council. And I thought you'd be perfect for our board."

"What makes you think that?" Chuck studied his colleague, feeling a little suspicious. "Do they need a CPA?"

"Well, we already have a couple of accountants. But I still think you'd be good."

"How long is a board term?"

"Not sure really. Not long though. Two... no, three years, I think."

"How does it work? I mean, who nominates me and when's the election held?"

"Think it's our committee." Henry grinned. "And I think the election's real soon. Don't worry, it's a done deal if you want it. Whatta ya say?"

(What would you say?)

HOW DO YOU ELECT YOUR BOARD MEMBERS?

Before your Board Development Committee goes galloping off, it really needs to know how the organization currently chooses its board members. The board audit will provide that very basic information. Here is where you find out how your organization "says" it goes about nominating and electing its board; and how its current board is comprised.

The audit begins with a review of the organization's policies on board membership: number, terms, configuration, nominating and elections, as reflected in the bylaws. It will also confirm the current number of board members, classifications represented, history rating of current members and demographics: gender, geographics, ethnic/multicultural and age. The informal audit will be a valuable resource document for those who will be charged with creating and managing the board development program. See Figure 1.4 for the Audit Worksheet.

Audit of Current
Board Elective Process *Worksheet*

THE AUDIT

Among the first tasks to be undertaken by the Board Development Committee and staff will be an audit of organizational policies on board membership and a review of current board make-up. The audit is an information gathering activity. It looks at each organizational factor which will have a bearing on creating a board leadership strategy. Compile the following information, which will be a valuable resource document as the board development process moves forward:

BYLAWS

Our organizational bylaws reflect the following about board membership: ✔

➔ **Number**: the numerical range or specific number of Board members shall be:_____

    ☐ Our bylaws do not state a specific range or number of board members.

    ☐ A bylaws amendment on range/number of board members is recommended.

Suggested amendment: _____

_____

    ☐ No amendment is necessary or recommended.

➔ **Board Terms:** the length of a board term shall be _____ years.

    ☐ Our bylaws do not stipulate the length of a board term.

    ☐ A bylaws amendment on board terms is recommended.

Suggested amendment: _____

_____

    ☐ No amendment is necessary or recommended.

➔ **Term Limits:** concurrent years of board service shall be limited to _____ years.

    ☐ Our bylaws do not stipulate limits to length of concurrent board service.

    ☐ A bylaws amendment on board term limits and rotation is recommended.

Suggested amendment: _____

_____

    ☐ No amendment is necessary or recommended.

FIGURE 1.4 ©1996 C3 Publications

➜ **Qualifications:** our bylaws include a statement of qualifications for board members: yes ☐ no ☐ (Refer to Figure 2.1, page 25, for a Model Statement of Qualifications)

   ☐ A bylaws amendment on qualifications for board service is recommended.

Suggested amendment: _____

_____

_____

   ☐ No amendment is necessary or recommended.

➜ **Nomination/election** procedures, as stated in our bylaws, are thorough, clear and complete: yes ☐ no ☐

   ☐ A bylaws amendment on nominating/election procedures is recommended.

Suggested amendment: _____

_____

_____

   ☐ No amendment is necessary or recommended.

➜ **Issues of representation** (geographic, professional, gender, ethnic, etc.), as stated in our bylaws, are thorough, clear and complete: yes ☐ no ☐

   ☐ A bylaws amendment on community representation is recommended.

Suggested amendment: _____

_____

_____

   ☐ No amendment is necessary or recommended.

➜ **Other relevant board membership issues stated in our bylaws are:**

_____

_____

_____

_____

_____

_____

_____

_____

_____

FIGURE 1.4 ©*1996 C3 Publications*

9

BOARD PROFILE

Complete the Board Profile Grid Form before taking next steps.
(See Appendix A for grid form, page 77)

➔ Our current number of active board members is: _____

Number Of Current Board Members By Business/ Professional Classification

Finance _____	Law _____
Government _____	Planning _____
Corporate Mgmt. _____	Marketing _____
Media _____	Health/Medicine _____
Education _____	Technology _____
Public Relations _____	Human Resource Management _____

_____ ____
(Other)

_____ ____
(Other)

_____ ____
(Other)

_____ ____
(Other)

_____ ____
(Other)

_____ ____
(Other)

Breakdown of Current Board History / Experience Rating

➔ Years on board (number each level): _____ 0-1   _____ 2-3
_____ 4-6   _____ 6+

➔ Number of board members who have served on one or more committees: _____   Number who have not: _____

➔ Number of board members who have served as officers: _____

➔ Number of directors who will cycle off board: This year _____
Next year _____

Demographic Breakdown of Current Board

➔ Gender (number): Male _____   Female _____

➔ Age (est. number each level): _____ 25-40   _____ 41-55
_____ 56-65   _____ 66+

➔ Ethnic / multicultural / minority groups (number represented): _____

FIGURE 1.4 ©*1996 C3 Publications*

→ Geographic breakdown (relevant to our organization):

_____

_____

_____

_____

_____

_____

OTHER BOARD AUDIT DATA

(add any related information deemed relevant to the board development audit):

_____

_____

_____

_____

_____

_____

IMPORTANT! *Make Changes Now.*

Correcting any determined deficiencies identified during the course of this audit should be considered before engaging in a board development strategy. For example, if your organization has no term limit policy, but sentiment is that there should be such a policy, a bylaws amendment should be made before recruiting new board members. Look at such issues separately and correct those which could confuse the board development process.

FIGURE 1.4 ©*1996 C3 Publications*

11

Assessing Organizational Readiness for the Task

CASE IN POINT ⇨

As the Smith County Youth Center monthly board meeting was coming to a close, Bob, the Board President, had one more item of business—something not on the agenda.

"Before we adjourn," he said, "we need to discuss board vacancies. It's been brought to my attention by staff that we will be four directors shy of our 15 minimum by the annual meeting."

Courtney was surprised. "That means we're losing over 25 percent of the board. What happened?"

Bob shrugged. "Sort of crept up on us. Two directors' terms are up. Jim, and you, too, Mary. Kevin has taken a new job out-of-state—and Jennifer resigned."

"Ouch!" said Ralph. As President-Elect he hadn't anticipated a sudden leadership gap. "And the annual meeting is what—five weeks or so away? Seems like a tight squeeze to me, Bob. And we're all busy anyway. Why not turn it over to staff," he said, looking at Elaine, the Executive Director, who was feeling her own responsibilities on the subject.

"Elaine will have input, of course, but it's mainly our job. We can parcel this out among ourselves. We know the kind of board members we want. And we all have contacts. Right?"

Grudging nods.

Bob nods back. " Okay. So here's what we'll do. Each of us give this some thought. Think of people you know. Flip through your Rolodexes and come up with two or three names. "I guarantee we will have this thing done in three or four weeks—well ahead of the annual meeting. Everybody agreed?"

(How about you? Would you agree?)

GOOD PEOPLE VS. GREAT BOARDS

Variations of the above scenario happen regularly within not-for-profit board rooms. Those organizations may then wonder why their boards never quite click; never quite connect with the mission, have a clear vision or get around to real planning. Maybe they have good people, but not great boards.

Whether replacing or adding members, the process should be conducted with thought. Too often, as our little story demonstrates, organizations merely declare the need for new board members and begin recruiting with no plan. Before asking a single person to consider joining a board, an assessment of readiness is the next order of business.

AN ASSESSMENT OF READINESS WILL CONSIDER THE FOLLOWING:

- Where is the organization going?

- Is it entering a new phase or proceeding with current plans?

- Have current board skills been compared to needs?

- What skills, experience and influence will be needed to carry the mission forward in the next five years?

- Is the organization *really* prepared to invite fresh leadership to join its board?

- Have current board members been asked to rate how they were recruited by your organization? What could be learned from such an exercise?

With the help of staff, a thorough assessment of your organization's readiness for board development need not be a lengthy process. See Figures 1.5 and 1.6, for the Assessment Worksheet and Board Culture Survey Form. Assessment and Survey results will be very useful as you prepare your development plan.

Assessment
of Readiness *Worksheet*

Assessing an organization's readiness to recruit new board members is one of the keys to success. Before approaching even one prospect, answering the following questions will help create a solid foundation of readiness upon which to base your board development plan:

1) Why are we engaging in a Board Development Program at this time?

✔ *(check all which apply)*

☐ Our organization has lost a number of board members recently.

☐ Several board members will soon reach their term limits.

☐ Certain deficiencies in board capability have been identified.

☐ Recent attention to future vision will call for board changes.

☐ Board development is simply an ongoing responsibility.

☐ Other reasons are:

_____

_____

2) Where is our organization going? ✔

Have we reviewed our mission statement in the last year? ☐ Yes ☐ No

If yes, was it confirmed? ☐ Yes ☐ No   Revised? ☐ Yes ☐ No

Have we engaged in strategic planning in the past 2 years? ☐ Yes ☐ No

Do we know what we want to accomplish in the next 5 years? ☐ Yes ☐ No

Have we revised/created our case statement in the past 2 years? ☐ Yes ☐ No

Does the board discuss our mission and vision regularly? ☐ Yes ☐ No

Is there a sense that we have a commonly held vision? ☐ Yes ☐ No

Other observations about the general direction of the organization:

_____

_____

_____

FIGURE 1.5 ©1996 C3 Publications

3) Where do we stand? ✔

Is our organization primarily maintaining established programs and procedures, as opposed to new strategies? ☐ Yes ☐ No

Is our organization engaged in implementing strategies established within the past 3 years? ☐ Yes ☐ No

Is our organization currently engaged in designing new strategies to be implemented in the near future? ☐ Yes ☐ No

Is there a sense of energy and focus about current or pending organizational strategies to fulfill our mission? ☐ Yes ☐ No

4) Comparing Board Skill to Leadership Needs ✔

Have we compared current board skills to leadership needs for the immediate and near (3-5 yr.) future? ☐ Yes ☐ No

If the answer to above question is no, address this step as part of the assessment. Refer again to the "Board Profile Grid" (Appendix A, page 77) completed as part of "Board Audit" for essential assessment information.

What board skills, experience and influence will be needed to meet organizational goals over the next 5 years? How will we integrate board development goals with our organization's strategic and/or long-range plan?

Note: Discuss questions addressed in 1-4 above with your Board Development Committee, gain consensus on leadership needs, then list them below:

Skills:_____

_____

Experience:_____

_____

Influence:_____

_____

Demographics:_____

_____

_____

FIGURE 1.5 ©*1996 C3 Publications*

15

5) Housekeeping: *Are We Prepared To Invite New Members To Join Our Board?*

One of the most important, and often overlooked, steps in assessing readiness for board development comes under "housekeeping". Quite simply, has the organization examined its closet to see what nagging issues may be languishing there? For example, do the bylaws need review, e.g., cleaning up a term limits policy? Is there a board job description; current, clear and specific? As part of this assessment, discuss the following assertions and any others needing clarification:

■ **The Bylaws** ✔

Do our bylaws contain any ambiguities or deficiencies which may have a bearing on board service? ☐ Yes ☐ No

If the answer to the above question is yes, how will these issues be addressed and remedied, and by what time?

_____

_____

■ **Board Job Description** ✔

Do we have a board job description? ☐ Yes ☐ No

If yes, is it comprehensive with clear expectations? ☐ Yes ☐ No

Has the job description been reviewed/revised recently? ☐ Yes ☐ No

If any of the answers to the above questions are no, how will these issues be addressed and remedied, and by what time?

_____

_____

■ **Board Staff / Relationship** ✔

Is our board clear about its role with regard to its relationship with the Chief Executive and other staff? ☐ Yes ☐ No

Has our board reviewed this subject at least annually? ☐ Yes ☐ No

Has there been misunderstandings by board members about their role, i.e., management vs. governance? ☐ Yes ☐ No

If any answers to the above reflect unfinished issues, how will they be addressed and remedied, and by what time? (See Appendices B & C, pages 79 & 80)

_____

_____

■ Board Policies ✔

Does our board have a conflict of interest policy? ☐ Yes ☐ No

Do we have appropriate financial policies and have they been recently reviewed and/or updated? ☐ Yes ☐ No

Do we have general operations & policies guidelines spelled out and readily available to the Board? ☐ Yes ☐ No

If any answers to the above questions are no, how will these issues be addressed and remedied, and by what time?

_____

_____

■ Internal Issues

Does our organization need to address other issues before we invite new members from the community to join our board?

— Keep in mind that an organization's image and reputation are significantly affected by how new people are brought onto a not-for-profit board, and by the issues which face them when they arrive.

— Any critical factors, i.e., budget deficit, consternation on the board, a recent internal crisis of any kind, pending major funding appeal — all of these need to be reviewed.

— The Board Development Committee should discuss any such factors candidly. If committee members are not fully informed on these matters, the chair should inquire and bring full details to the table.

— It is unethical for an organization to invite unsuspecting individuals onto a board without fully informing them of critical issues.

— What internal concerns do we need to review? How will we manage their resolution or interpretation?

_____

_____

6) Other

Often, through the process of the information audit and the readiness assessment, other questions are triggered. Committee members should be queried by the chair regarding any other concerns, observations or suggestions they may have. Any significant ideas or questions should be considered by the committee and added to the text of this assessment.

_____

_____

FIGURE 1.5 ©*1996 C3 Publications*

17

Gauging Your
Board Culture *Survey Form*

Part of assessing organizational readiness is evaluating your own board culture on the subject of recruitment. How do your current members rate their personal experiences? How were they brought into the organization? It is important to gauge how acting directors feel on this subject—and to use what is learned to enhance the work of the Board Development Committee.

Seek input from your current board members by asking them to share their experience and opinions about how they came to be on your Board of Directors.

BOARD FEEDBACK SURVEY ✔

1. How long have you served on the board ? _____ Years

2. Briefly describe the circumstances which led you to join our board ?

   _____

   _____

   _____

   _____

3. What steps in our recruitment process would you rate highly?

   _____

   _____

   _____

   _____

4. What steps in our recruitment process do you feel need improvement?

   _____

   _____

   _____

   _____

FIGURE 1.6 ©1996 C3 Publications

5. During the recruitment process, were you adequately informed about the organization, i.e., our mission, activities, financial affairs, and what your role would be as a member of the board? ☐ Yes ☐ Mostly ☐ No

   — If "No" or "Mostly," how did we fail to meet your needs or expectations?

   _____

   _____

6. Were you given an orientation following your election to the board?
   ☐ Yes ☐ No

   — If "Yes", did this introduction adequately help you get your bearings and gain the information necessary to begin your board service? ☐ Yes ☐ No
   — If "No", how could we improve our orientation efforts?

   _____

   _____

7. Subsequent to your election to the board, did you receive adequate training and support for your duties on the board and for other activities in which you were asked to participate? ☐ Yes ☐ No

   — If "No", how could we improve our orientation efforts?

   _____

   _____

8. Please provide any suggestions regarding our board development, recruitment, and training process which you feel may assist your colleagues on the Board Development Committee. Thank you for your input.

   _____

   _____

   _____

   _____

   _____

   Name (optional): _____

FIGURE 1.6 ©*1996 C3 Publications*

SECTION 2

GAME PLAN STRATEGIES

"The crucial point in the board membership process is when the candidate is approached with, 'We need you!' The candidate usually responds: 'What for?' What for! In the answer to this question lies the key to recruiting a board member, to an effective board, and in the long term, to a successful voluntary organization."

—*William R. Conrad*

Creating the Board Development Plan

....

D o n ' t   e n d   u p

s o m e p l a c e   e l s e

As the saying goes: "If you don't know where you are going, you're likely to end up someplace else." Nothing could be truer when it comes to board development. Even more costly, if you don't know where you're going, you may not *know* you have ended up someplace else. Someplace with much less potential than you had envisioned.

Once the Board Development Committee has completed the audit and assessment steps, it is time to begin creating an actual plan. With the results of the two research activities, the committee will have up-to-date, accurate information upon which to base its action plan. The plan need not be voluminous; in fact, it should be a concise, even lean, outline of specific steps to build and sustain a healthy, effective board.

The plan should include realistic goals based on an achievable time frame, specific recruitment objectives and any other criteria which may help drive the process. The essential elements of a plan can be created using the Development Plan Worksheet. See Figure 2.1.

Where do you look for board members? The first rule of board recruitment is: "Do not clone yourselves." Obviously, you need to look within your internal constituency for prospects or leads to prospects among: the current board, organizational committees, other volunteers and staff. In fact, developing board members through committee experience is often a very good process. Just don't limit your search to that internal core group.

You should also consider your external constituency *(donors and friends)* and others who know you and support your organization but are not active internally. In fact, the primary opportunity to turn donors into major givers is involvement through board membership.

THE SUCCESSFUL BOARD DEVELOPMENT PLAN IS BASED ON:

- thoughtful assessment,
- a realistic game plan,
- and an investment of time to do the research, the contact work and decision-making.

These steps will give greater assurance that you will be able to find and attract the best people from your community to serve on the board. That means looking inside, outside—everywhere it takes to end up with a board which is balanced, competent, committed and visionary.

The Development Plan *Worksheet*

The plan you are about to create will be the "linchpin" to your board development goals. It will be based on your preparation thus far, and provide the template for your actual recruitment strategies. The effort you put into your plan, and your commitment to process beyond the plan, will make the difference.

1) Revisiting the Board Development Committee

The audit and assessment steps may have revealed the need for additional committee skills, knowledge or special qualifications. Now, before the actual work plan is crafted, is the time to add additional members if needed. It can be distracting and can slow committee progress if membership is changed mid-course.

2) Qualifications for Board Membership

From the IRS to the state attorney general and donors, community boards are being held to a higher standard. A statement of board qualifications will help assure that the board created is one of competence, commitment and high ethical standards. Points of expertise to consider are: previous NFP board experience, knowledge of fiduciary responsibility, understanding of governance duties/process, knowledge of your organization's mission and perhaps specific skill-sets, e.g., attorney, CPA. Expertise, however, needs the balance of such traits as fairness, sense of stewardship, commitment to what is right, respect for the role of colleagues and staff, ability to work with others, and a passion to serve. Additional qualifications may include professional, geographical or demographic criteria. Examine your bylaws, board job description, or other documents for a statement of qualifications:

■ If your bylaws (or other document/s) already carry a statement of qualifications for board membership, review it for accuracy and relevance.

■ If your organization has no statement of qualifications for board membership, consider drafting one for board consideration and adoption. *(See the following as an example. Modify to fit your organization's profile.)*

MODEL STATEMENT OF QUALIFICATIONS:

The elected members of the Board of Directors shall consist of persons who are interested in the mission of the _____ , understand and accept their responsibilities of organizational governance and fiduciary oversight, and who are chosen for the purpose of providing the Board of Directors with the operational skills, ethical leadership, and personal commitment required to achieve the purpose and goals of the organization. The composition of the Board of Directors shall also reflect a geographical representation with one-third coming from _____ , one-third from _____ and the remaining one-third at large. Additionally, the Board of Directors will have no more than _____ members from the _____ professional sector, *(i.e., specific profession or other classification. Intent is to avoid imbalance of board members with certain vested interests. Too many health professionals on a health organization board, etc.).*

Note: In striving for balanced representation from the community and their constituency, organizations may occasionally face the necessity or opportunity of bringing less experienced members onto their boards. In those instances, the board will benefit from providing extra training opportunities so those members meet board qualifications and become informed decision-makers.

FIGURE 2.1 ©1996 C3 Publications

3) Creating the Plan

Board recruitment goals are more than mere numbers. Your plan is based on needs you have identified during the audit, and assessment exercises, and as may be found in your organization's strategic plan. As you begin to create your board development plan, keep the following resource documents close at hand: the audit, the Assessment, the Board Grid, your strategic plan.

■ **Step A — *Category "Targeting List":*** First, refer to previously identified leadership needs and create your board development goals by listing specific category "targets" below.

TARGETING LIST	
BOARD SLOT CATEGORIES*	**NUMBER**
Marketing / Public Relations	*2*

* **Board Slot Categories to consider are:** Career skills, personal characteristics, volunteer experience, gender, multicultural, age. (Refer to Figure 2.3 for Board Position Specifications Checklist.)

■ **Step B — *Setting the goals and a time frame:*** While maintaining a capable board is an ongoing, long-term process, in the short run it may be more effective to break down your annual goal into manageable "bites"— along with measurable objectives. In this case we are using 90-day time frames to achieve your annual goal.

Number: Our overall annual goal for additional board members shall total: _____

Annual Time Frame to meet our current board development goals shall be:

　　From: Month _____ Year _____　　**To:** Month _____ Year _____

90-Day Time Frame: Next, prioritize your category "targeting list" and transfer the information to the 90-Day Recruitment Goals Plan Schedule (see Figure 2.2). Enter your intended 90-day time frame in each of the columns provided, and insert your category goals accordingly. This process meshes your goals with your time frame and focused efforts on your most immediate needs.

FIGURE 2.1 ©*1996 C3 Publications*　　　　　　　　　　　　　　　　　　25

90-Day Recruitment Goals *PLAN SCHEDULE*

Board Slot Categories Prioritized from Targeting List	Number Per Category	GOALS PER 90-DAY TIME FRAME: Each column represents 90-days			
		1-From _____ to _____	2-From _____ to _____	3-From _____ to _____	4-From _____ to _____
Marketing / Public Relations	2	1		1	
90-DAY TOTALS →					

Board Position Specs *Checklist*

Use this checklist to help "round out" each board position you want to fill. Match the career/professional skills you want, with desired personal characteristics and prior organizational experience. For instance, say you have a board position focus of "marketing." The career skills you want for that position may be: media, business, public relations and marketing. Along with that you would like personal characteristics which include: the person is a doer, has certain access, and contacts. This person's volunteer experience would take in fund raising, special projects and that he/she is a good planner. Add to that the specific responsibilities you would like this candidate to assume and there you have it! A concise specification profile. *(Complete a checklist for each slot you will fill)*

BOARD POSITION FOCUS: _____

(e.g., financial expertise, advisor on legal matters, advertising/marketing background, computer skills)

✔ CAREER SKILLS BEING SOUGHT FOR THIS BOARD POSITION

☐ Marketing   ☐ Banking   ☐ Accounting   ☐ Business
☐ Insurance   ☐ Education   ☐ Health   ☐ PR
☐ Planning   ☐ Investments   ☐ Architecture   ☐ Religion
☐ Media   ☐ Government   ☐ Technology   ☐ Program
☐ Fund raising   ☐ Law   ☐ Human resources

☐ Other: _____

✔ PERSONAL CHARACTERISTICS BEING SOUGHT FOR THIS BOARD POSITION

☐ Community contacts   ☐ Access to assets   ☐ Access to desired "niche"
☐ Professional clout   ☐ Personal assets   ☐ Community influence
☐ Responsible   ☐ Leadership   ☐ Participates w/enthusiasm
☐ Is a "doer"   ☐ Team player   ☐ Is not over-extended

☐ Other: _____

✔ VOLUNTEER EXPERIENCE RATING BEING SOUGHT FOR THIS BOARD POSITION

☐ Prior board service   ☐ Board officer experience   ☐ Strategic planner
☐ Fund raising   ☐ Management expertise   ☐ Visionary
☐ Chairperson service   ☐ Has volunteer experience   ☐ Special projects
☐ Is a "doer"   ☐ Team player   ☐ Is not over-extended

☐ Other: _____

SPECIFIC RESPONSIBILITIES YOU WILL WANT THIS BOARD MEMBER TO ASSUME:

_____

_____

_____

Mid-Course Check ✔

··

H o w   w e   d o i n ' ?

CASE IN POINT ⇨

Rex agreed to serve on the Board Development Committee and was indeed committed to the goal of nurturing board leadership. But he was also used to a quick meeting of the Nominating Committee and, just as quickly, agreement around the committee table of who knew who and who would be asked to join the board.

He was "antsy" when he called Heather, the committee chair.

"Heather, I commend you for a very thorough approach to filling our board vacancies this year. I can really see the value. But can't we shortcut some of it? After all, we know what we want."

"Yes," she responded, "but do we really know 'who' we want?"

"Sure, you saw the list. We've got names."

(Cloning 101 raises its head.)

WARNING: *TIME-OUT! SYNCHRONIZE WATCHES!*

Ultimately, after the commitment, the audit, the assessment and the plan—it comes down to nuts-and-bolts recruiting. This is also a point where all of your hard work can become derailed. Without maintaining solid commitment to the process, and the intended outcome, your efforts can unravel if . . .

■ some committee members are anxious to cut to the chase and get on with it; want to start asking people—now !

■ others are feeling time pressures from work, or other demands, and want to go off on their own;

■ a few feel stifled by "process"—find it confining;

■ one or two struggle and become disheartened, perhaps feeling inadequate or even intimidated by the task.

AT THIS POINT, THE COMMITTEE LEADER . . .THE CHAMPION . . .

. . . needs to help the committee maintain a strict focus on the strategies previously agreed to. Keep everyone working together. The key is approaching the right people with a quality introduction to the organization. If the recruiting process appears to be in disarray, the impact on prospective board members will not be good. It is important that the chair maintain committee consensus on your recruitment plan and procedures.

THE MESSAGE

Stay on track. Make any needed course corrections. Rely on your thorough preparation and follow-through. Your efforts will yield positive results.

SECTION 3

RECRUITMENT
A-C-T-I-O-N !

"...trusteeship is serious business. It is not simply an honor. Nor is it simply attendance at luncheons and tea parties. It is an activity that requires knowledge, commitment and time."

—*Thomas Wolf*

Identifying Prospects

The volunteer

"draft"

A WORD HERE ABOUT INCLUSIVENESS

Consider all volunteers and staff as partners in identifying and suggesting new volunteers. Ask them to submit names of potential leadership prospects. While the actual number of eventual candidates coming from a general "call" may not be large, such inclusiveness strengthens the process. You never know who may have unique contacts in the community.

> **Note:** *Advise all staff and volunteers to submit names without contacting the person in question. This policy will avoid embarrassment if a prospect is not eventually invited to accept nomination to the board, join a committee or other post.*

However, the bulk of potential prospects will most likely come from the resources of the committee, leads from the Chief Executive and key staff, and research into other community sources: Chamber of Commerce, minority business or cultural organizations, civic clubs, community foundations, etc. Regardless of the source of the names, they should be thoroughly reviewed by the Board Development Committee before setting the recruitment slate.

Again, while it is tempting to talk to prospects before all of the preparatory work is completed, remember: it is hard, if not impossible, to "undo" an invitation, or even a general inquiry which hints of a possible invitation. Always keep the reputation of your organization in mind at each step along the way. And—respect the individual.

A CONTROLLED FREE-FOR-ALL!

The first step of identifying potential candidates is to engage in a controlled free-for-all, a volunteer "draft." Your committee will enjoy this exercise, akin to a football player draft. Each member develops a list of all of the names, and sources of names, they think are relevant to the development plan: possible prospects, known potential candidates, sources of prospects. See Figure 3.1, Volunteer "Draft" Worksheet. (**Note**: *Again, it is recommended that you not rely solely on the personal contacts of committee members.*)

Next, the names from all sources are listed on chart paper/chalkboard/white board, so all can see—comparing them to needs/goals identified earlier. Once all suggested names are listed, the process moves forward to the next step: qualifying the prospects into candidates.

The Volunteer "Draft" Worksheet

NAME	PROFESSION	COMPANY	FOR WHAT BOARD SLOT?	SOURCE	MOVE TO QUALIFY ?
Harry Smith	CPA	Price-Waterhouse	Finance/Budget	Mary Brown	Yes

COMMITTEE MEMBER: _____ DATE COMPLETED: _____

Beyond Nominating

FIGURE 3.1 ©*1996 C3 Publications*

Qualifying the Prospects

....

. . . into Candidates

CASE IN POINT ⇨

"Okay," said Stephen. "We've got a list of, let's see, nine, ten, eleven—eleven possible board candidates. We're home free. We can pick the three nominees we need and have it all done in one meeting."

Paul wasn't so sure. "Wait a minute. Shouldn't we see if these folks pass muster?"

"What for?" Stephen defended his position. "We know all of these folks, or at least one of us knows each of them. There's nothing to pass."

"I don't know about that, Steve." Marilyn pointed to one name on the list. "For instance, Mel, here, may not be available. I just heard that he's taken on a new assignment with his company. The word is 60 percent travel."

"That's what I mean," said Paul. "First off, no sense asking Mel to serve if we're pretty sure we'll get a turn down. And secondly, what if he said yes and then we never see him at any board meetings? Fat lot of good that would be."

"Okay, okay. But that's just one guy. A fluke. The rest look great. We'd be happy to get any one of them to serve on the board."

Marilyn wasn't convinced. "I still think Paul is right, Steve. We should really look at each of these names carefully. For instance, I just saw Cari a few days ago. She told me she was serving on six nonprofit boards. Six! With our game plan for a more responsive board, especially one more involved in fund raising, I don't think we should take on people who are over-committed."

Stephen raised his arms in mock surrender and laughed. "Okay. I give up! You're right. We sure don't want to do all of this work and end up with no shows and the like."

(Point made?)

CERTIFYING ELIGIBILITY ISN'T ABOUT BEING "STUFFY"

Once potential board candidates have been identified through the volunteer "draft," the next step is to "qualify" these prospects. Qualifying is the act of certifying—of declaring a person eligible, competent, and desirable for the specific assignments in question. In this case, to serve on the board and possibly accept a committee post.

■ Why qualify? *For two reasons:*

1) To actually assess a prospect's experience, skills, community access, influence, reputation, possible interest and availability;

2) To compare a prospect's skills and experience against the specific needs of the organization and then to prioritize those factors against a list of other prospects.

BE PATIENT, DON'T JUMP THE GUN!

Once again it is important to wait before extending invitations of nomination. For instance, say you have a goal of five new board members, but you have a qualified pool of 18 prospects. Our oft repeated caveat is still in effect. If any of the 18 are contacted prematurely, then somehow not selected, you risk embarrassment and damage to both organizational image and future recruiting efforts. Plus, you may miss getting the best prospects on your list because someone jumped the gun.

The act of qualifying prospects will require some personal effort and knowledge. All inquiries should be confidential and information gathered available only to the committee and Chief Executive. Much of the qualifying will take place at the committee table through exchange and discussion. Qualifying information can be transferred to an informational form. See Figure 3.2 for Prospective Board Candidate Form.

Prospective Board Candidate *F O R M*

C O N F I D E N T I A L ...   FOR COMMITTEE USE ONLY
NOT TO BE DISTRIBUTED

Name of Committee Member completing this form: _____

Date completed: _____ Phone: _____

Prospect Name: _____

Home Address: _____

City / State: _____ Zip: _____ Phone: _____

Business Name: _____

Title: _____ Phone: _____

Bus. Mailing Address: _____

City / State: _____ Zip: _____

Business / Profession: _____

Skills of interest to our organization: _____

_____

Activities that would interest this person: _____

_____

Any previous experience with our organization: (*List activities, dates if known*)

_____

Past volunteer experience with other organizations: _____

_____

Current level of volunteer commitment with other organizations *(number, boards)*.

_____

_____

State why you think this individual would be an asset to the board of directors and our organization overall.

_____

_____

_____

State any factors which you feel may detract from this individual's ability to serve as a board member or in other volunteer posts with our organization *(overcommitted with other organizations, job responsibilities, other)*.

_____

_____

_____

Please suggest who should make the first contact with this prospect to arrange an exploratory meeting regarding leadership development.

_____

Please suggest who should attend the exploratory meeting *(i.e., yourself, the Chief Executive, the Board President, others - no more than two persons)*.

_____

If you know what times, dates and locations might be preferable, or would best accommodate this prospect, please indicate.

_____

_____

Note: If you have additional comments or information which will be useful in the consideration and recruitment of this prospect, please add here.

_____

_____

_____

_____

_____

   FIGURE 3.2   ©1996 C3 Publications

Setting the Slate & Making the Dates !

CASE IN POINT ⇨

The Community Health Clinic's Nominating Committee was basking in a sense of accomplishment. Their prospect selection efforts had paid off with a strong list of potential board candidates.

"We've done well, my friends," said Joel, running his finger down the page. "Any one of these folks would make a good addition to the board."

As committee chair, Susan was pleased. "I feel good about this group, too. Now we need to make personal contact with each one—finish it up right."

Stan cleared his throat; he wasn't so sure. "I've been thinking about that," he said. "I don't really see the need to go through all that fuss on these personal visits, and follow-ups."

"You're kidding, Stan," said Joel. "After all of this work you want to stop short of success?"

"No. We can simply send each of them a letter and get their decision with a follow-up phone call. Save a bunch of time—theirs and ours. Anyway, most of us either know these people or have a referral name. Not exactly a cold call."

Susan wasn't convinced. "That's like planting your garden and watering it from a helicopter at 10,000 feet. Stan, your letter and phone call are a good way to set up an appointment. But I think this is about people connecting with people, face-to-face."

(Susan is right.)

IT'S ALL ABOUT REAL PEOPLE

The strategic steps *(assessing, planning and selection)* are primarily "tactical," but once prospects have been qualified as potential candidates, the subsequent steps are "personal." Now you enter the people phase: confirming a slate of "real" people, making that first person-to-person contact, *(albeit letter or phone call)* and then actually sitting down with them face-to-face.

After all of your thoughtful work to create an exceptional pool of prospective candidates, the key to success hinges finally on a "personal approach." In spite of Stan's sense of efficiency, recruiting someone to accept a board position from arms length is, at best, cursory. Beyond that, however, it could be viewed as insensitive, disrespectful—even arrogant. It would be unethical to ask a person to accept board appointment without full disclosure and without assessing the person's capability to serve. And that calls for personal connection.

GETTING READY FOR THE FIRST DATE

Once the qualification process has been completed, it is time to prioritize the names, set the actual slate of prospects to be approached, and decide who should make the initial contact:

- Review all of the qualified names brought to the table.

- Compare and confirm them again to the needs of the organization *(refer to audit and assessment—and long-range or strategic plans as may be applicable).*

- Prioritize prospects and select the top names to be approached *(set number).*

- Review remaining names, prioritize and retain for future board recruitment and as possible prospects for committees or projects.

- The committee ratifies its selections and formally agrees on the "first level" recruitment slate. See Figure 3.3. for "Slate & Dates" Appointment Worksheet.

- Reminder: Keep all names and the status of selection process confidential to eliminate misinformation from being passed along.

"Slate & Dates" *Worksheet*

LIST NAME OF PROSPECTS IN PRIORITY ORDER

	Prospect	Contact Person	Date 1st Meeting	Proceed Y or N	Closure Contact/s	Date 2nd Meeting	Status Y/N/Other
①	John Doe	Mary Smith	Oct. 10	Yes	Chief Exec & Mary Smith	Dec. 5	Yes
②							
③							
④							
⑤							
⑥							
⑦							
⑧							
⑨							
⑩							

Notes

_____

_____

_____

_____

Approach · Message · Role

Clarifying
Your Story

WHAT'S THE APPROACH?

Before making those first appointments for lunch or coffee, it is important that the committee is certain of its approach. Are you going to contact each person only about "board" membership, or are you going to discuss a search for new "leadership" for the organization? What will you do if, for some reason, a candidate doesn't seem to be ready, suited or available for board service? You may want to steer them to a committee, or have to disengage in a respectful manner. Clarify your general approach before people are contacted.

WHAT'S THE MESSAGE?

What will be the story each prospect is told? In addition to explaining the organization's mission, programs and services—why are new volunteers being sought? Each committee member needs to be clear and feel comfortable with the message to be given. Be pro-active, you are: entering an exciting new phase, addressing a challenging future vision, seeking new volunteers to work with existing leadership to sustain the progress of the organization. However, if there are organizational issues needing attention, don't hold that back. These prospects may be the ones to help resolve such matters. Be candid. Become comfortable with why you are engaged in volunteer development. It is important that there be agreement and clarity in creating the message. See Figure 3.4 for Creating the Message Worksheet.

WHAT WILL THEY DO?

Committee members should possess information about typical duties of volunteers: committees, fund raising, the board—and be able to relate it informally, but clearly, to prospects. Each committee member should also be familiar with the board job description and be able to relate general board duties, even though the printed job description may not be given to the prospect at the first meeting. The goal is to provide selected information at each step: introduction, invitation and orientation; enough that the prospect is informed, but not buried. See Appendix D, page 82, for Model Board Job Description.

Creating the Message *Worksheet*

....

Informing the
Candidates

What will the Board Development Committee, Board President, Chief Executive and others involved say to potential candidates? Your core message should be focused, clear and concise. Taking time to create a message which provides basic information, speaks to the essence of your organization's mission and future vision, and deals with special circumstances, will pay dividends later.

SELECTING THE CONTENT, *CREATING THE MESSAGE*

■ The Organization

What are the essential facts we wish to convey, generally, about our organization when approaching prospective candidates?

History: _____

Mission: _____

Organizational structure: _____

Programs & Services: _____

Special circumstances: _____
(pending capital campaign, possible merger, other unique circumstances)

Other: _____

■ Fiscal Affairs

What financial information should be relayed about our organization to prospects at various stages of the recruitment process?

Annual Report with financial statement: _____

Annual budget: _____

Annual audit: _____

Statement of fiscal stability: _____

Special circumstances: _____
(loss of major funding source, unique debt load, major expansion of services)

Other: _____

FIGURE 3.4 ©*1996 C3 Publications*   *41*

■ Financial Development

What fund raising and resource development practices and activities should be outlined at each stage of recruitment?

Sources of funding: _____

Board role in resource development:_____

Individual member role: _____

Special circumstances: _____
(pending major funding drive, new strategic funding goals, unique expectations)

Other:_____

■ Organizational Operations

What information about how our organization operates on a day-to-day basis should be provided to candidates?

Departments: _____

Committees: _____

Staffing:_____

Special circumstances: _____
(major staff change, organizational restructuring, unique committee issues)

Other:_____

■ Board of Directors

What essential elements should be presented regarding the role and responsibilities of the board, and at what stage of the recruitment process?

Governance: _____

Personal commitment: _____

Committee participation: _____

Financial development: _____

Individual responsibilities:_____

Mutual expectations: _____

Leadership development: _____

General representation of organization: _____

Special circumstances: _____
(board culture: how you operate, any dysfunction being dealt with, unique issues)

Other:_____

FIGURE 3.4 ©1996 C3 Publications

■ Planning

What information regarding various planning activities and goals of the organization should be shared with candidates?

Long-range strategic plan: _____

Financial development plan: _____

Operations plan: _____

Technology plans: _____

Marketing plans: _____

Future vision objectives: _____

Special circumstances:_____
(plans in progress, no planning has been done, about to begin planning)

Other: _____

■ Board Development

What message should be given to prospects regarding the current board development/recruitment activities?

Transition of board leadership: _____

Future vision needs:_____

Ongoing leadership development: _____

Specific skills/talents needs: _____

Specific knowledge of community:_____

Specific organizational objectives: _____

Special circumstances:_____
(major new strategies, internal issues of change, leadership issues)

Other: _____

■ Oh, By The Way —*Just what will they be doing?*

When all is said and done, each candidate will want to know, with some specificity, what they "personally" will be doing as a board member. In addition to "the core message," be prepared to give them some examples of possible assignments. Encouraging candidates to serve beyond their board duties will help assure their investment and enjoyment of being a volunteer, such as:

FIGURE 3.4 ©*1996 C3 Publications*

43

Board standing committees: _____

Service or program committees:_____

Fund raising committees: _____

Special project committees: _____

Special event committees: _____

Other: _____

CREATING THE MESSAGE AND *"LEANING OUT"* THE CONTENT

After confirming the information you have decided to include in your message to prospective candidates, prioritize it. Hone it down. Distill it into absolutely the leanest form you can and still present the core message. Next, craft that list of priorities into a one or two page message of essentials. That statement will then be the anchor message upon which each committee member can base his/her conversations with the prospects/candidates.

ORGANIZATIONAL INFORMATION

Next, what specific printed information should be provided to each prospect at the various stages of the recruitment process? Consider creating three packets to be given out at different times during the recruitment process.

CHECK ITEMS TO BE INCLUDED ✔

	Introductory	Invitation	Orientation
■ Mission statement	☐	☐	☐
■ Future vision statement	☐	☐	☐
■ General information fact sheet	☐	☐	☐
■ Selected brochures	☐	☐	☐
■ Organizational history	☐	☐	☐
■ Newsletter	☐	☐	☐
■ Annual report	☐	☐	☐
■ Annual audit	☐	☐	☐
■ Organizational bylaws	☐	☐	☐
■ Minutes of board meetings	☐	☐	☐
■ Current financial report	☐	☐	☐
■ Board roster	☐	☐	☐
■ Staff roster	☐	☐	☐
■ Organizational chart	☐	☐	☐
■ Board job description	☐	☐	☐
■ Confirm officers/directors insurance	☐	☐	☐
■ Calendar of future board meetings	☐	☐	☐

FIGURE 3.4 ©1996 C3 Publications

	Introductory	Invitation	Orientation
■ Calendar of upcoming events/activities	☐	☐	☐
■ List of organizational committees	☐	☐	☐
■ Board manual	☐	☐	☐
■ Policies & procedures manual	☐	☐	☐
■ Organizational strategic plan	☐	☐	☐
■ Financial development plan	☐	☐	☐
■ Marketing plan	☐	☐	☐
■ Case statement	☐	☐	☐
■ Executive director résumé	☐	☐	☐

OTHER

	Introductory	Invitation	Orientation
■ _____	☐	☐	☐
■ _____	☐	☐	☐
■ _____	☐	☐	☐
■ _____	☐	☐	☐
■ _____	☐	☐	☐
■ _____	☐	☐	☐
■ _____	☐	☐	☐
■ _____	☐	☐	☐

INFORMATION PACKETS

Once the committee has selected the printed materials it wants to share with prospects, using different packets can help keep information flow clear:

PACKET A: Contains information to be used at the introductory level.

PACKET B: Contains information to aid a candidate in making his/her decision regarding your organization's invitation to join the Board.

PACKET C: Contains information to be disseminated at an orientation session.

GIVE A GOOD IMPRESSION

Put the information in a portfolio with the organization's logo, or one prepared for that purpose. The packet should be attractive, but not gaudy, and contain essential information for each phase of the recruitment process. Do not overload prospects with paper. A portfolio bulging with pamphlets and brochures will overwhelm the prospect and not make a good impression.

FIGURE 3.4 ©*1996 C3 Publications*

45

Time for Action

Getting to the Ask

RECRUITMENT—*OUT ON THE STREETS!*

After the initial prospect slate and recruitment procedures have been set and prioritized by the committee, it is time to move out into the community. Remember, stay with the top priority list until all on that list have been confirmed or eliminated before moving on to the next priority level of prospects. Refer to Figure 3.3 "Slate & Dates" Appointment Worksheet.

THE COMMITTEE CONFIRMS:

- who will make the initial contact with each candidate;
- who will arrange a face-to-face meeting;
- who will attend the first meeting;
- and when those actions will take place.

In most cases, the first contact will be undertaken by the person who knows them best, or has some sort of entree with the person's employer or on some other basis. In other instances, it may be best for the Board President and Chief Executive to initiate the contact on referral of a committee member or other party. Use whichever approach seems most appropriate.

HOT PROSPECTS—*WHAT NEXT?*

Once the initial meetings have occurred, the committee will need to confirm which prospects will become priority candidates. For the priority candidates who are interested, it will then be time to bring in the organizational leadership if that hasn't already happened. The President, Chief Executive, selected board officers or others, need to take the lead from the committee and set up a face-to-face meeting with each candidate who is ready for the next step. "Next step" meaning that they are still interested, seem to have the "right stuff" for the organization's mission and are deemed to add strength and capability to the organization. Here is where all of the planning and research is put to the test.

CLOSURE—*THE ASK*

This is what you have been working for—the ask. It is time to bring the process to closure. Closure will mean that the candidate is fully briefed on what his or her duties would be as a board member, is provided with a board job description, bylaws, financial reports and other pertinent information. The candidate is also informed about expected time commitments and overall involvement. If their interest is confirmed, and they are qualified, an invitation is extended to accept nomination to the board *(appointment to a committee or other outcome)*. Upon acceptance by the candidate, every effort is made to answer any remaining questions the person may have, provide them with additional information they request, inform them of what the next steps will be *(i.e., election, first board meeting they will attend, committee appointment, orientation, etc.)*, and fill in any gaps. See Figure 3.5 for The Art of the Ask Guidelines.

The Art of the Ask *Guidelines*

Before approaching a prospective board candidate, it is important that several factors be confirmed prior to face-to-face meetings and an eventual invitation:

1) Who makes the contact?

Once a prospect is identified, and confirmed as a prime candidate, who should make the initial contact? See Figure 3.3 for "Slate & Dates" Appointment Worksheet.

2) How should the contact be made?

A personal phone call to set up an appointment? By letter, indicating a follow-up phone call to set an appointment? By introduction of a third party, followed by a letter or phone call? Think through the options of the introductory contact; select the best option for each prospect and proceed.

Note: Do not leave candidates in the dark. Let them know that you want to talk about the organization's leadership development efforts. Tell them that their name has been recommended as a potential volunteer candidate and you want to meet informally with them to discuss the possibilities. No obligation; just informal.

(Caveat: At this point be clear if actual board candidacy is going to be mentioned. If you do and for some reason a person doesn't seem appropriate, i.e., he/she is over-committed, less experienced than previously thought, agrees but seems lukewarm, it could become embarrassing—or the organization may end up with a poor board member. Consider in advance how you are going to handle those conditions should they arise.)

3) Who should attend this "First Date?"

Should it only be the person who makes the initial contact? Or should that person partner with another; perhaps the Board President or the Chief Executive? If so, why? Will the addition of the second person add significantly to this first meeting? In what way?

Note: Unless the candidate indicates that he or she will be bringing a guest, it is probably not advisable to have more than two people from the organization attend this first meeting. In most cases, one-on-one will work best. But in the end, it is a judgment call.

4) How will the introductory meeting proceed?

It will be important that the person representing your organization be clear about his or her role. The initial approach will be important to the candidate. Your representative should be prepared to introduce the organization in a simple, yet informative, manner; neither too much nor too little information should be "dumped" on the prospect at this point. The message should have been determined in advance by the committee so that each member is giving the same clear message. See Figure 3.4 for Creating the Message Worksheet.

FIGURE 3.5 ©*1996 C3 Publications*

47

CONSIDERATIONS FOR THE INTRODUCTORY MEETING

- *Explain very simply that the organization is in the process of enhancing its base of volunteer leadership.*

- *Tell the candidate that he/she has been selected by the organization's leadership development committee as a person who would add strength to the organization's volunteer base.*

- *Introduce the organization's mission and programs, concisely; with enough information for the candidate to grasp the scope of purpose, activities, and services of your organization. Have information you can leave with the candidate.* See Figure 3.4, i.e., information packets.

- *In general, but clear terms, tell the candidate the type of responsibilities he or she may encounter as a volunteer. It is permissible at this juncture to be more general. If the person indicates interest, the next meeting with organizational leaders will provide more definitive details; and indeed they must declare all pertinent facts. Of course there is no need to drag out the process if everything is clicking, especially if the candidate is well-known, highly desirable — in essence "pre-approved."*

5) How long should the first meeting last?

If the meeting is in the candidate's office, or over a cup of coffee, 30 minutes is about the right length of time. Over lunch, one hour would an appropriate time. Use your best judgment, it will depend on the parties involved.

Ask the person if you may schedule 20-30 minutes of their time. Let them know, in advance, how much time the meeting will take from their day. Then, respect that agreement. The same goes for lunch; if they give you an hour, be prepared to wrap things up in that time. If the prospect seems a good match, make sure you pin down the next step—see #6 below. Find out when would be a good time for them to meet with the Board President and Chief Executive *(or other leadership)*. Get two or three date and time options.

6) From prospect to candidate

If the prospect expresses interest in joining your organization as a volunteer, a second meeting should be suggested. At this point, the Board President, Chief Executive and/or a committee chair *(whichever seems most appropriate)* should meet with the prospect. This does two things: 1) It shows the candidate that they are respected and considered important to the organization; 2) It brings the most knowledgeable people together with the prospect, people who should be able to answer any and all questions and who can interpret the ins and outs of the organization with clarity. And by now, it has been made clear that you are seeking the prospect's interest in board candidacy. If all is going well, the person being recruited is ready to "be asked" at this meeting. You may also want to consider holding this second meeting on-site, at your organization's offices or facility. Especially if you have some show-and-tell capability, or even if you just want the person to gain a sense of "place".

FIGURE 3.5 ©*1996 C3 Publications*

7) The Ask

"We would like you to consider our formal invitation to accept nomination to the Board of Directors." Make the ask and be ready to answer any questions which will be brought out by the actual invitation. Questions like: "What is the time commitment?" "What will be my specific duties?" "When do you meet?" "Will I have to raise money?" "I don't know much about your mission, will there be some training?" Answer all questions. Come prepared to provide details: financial status, core services and programs, and intended volunteer responsibilities. The future direction of the organization should be discussed, challenges being faced, and likely activities in which the prospect will be involved. Promise to get back to them with any questions you can't answer on the spot. *(Be sure and do it.)*

8) Be very clear about what will happen next

Once a prospect has accepted the invitation, be clear about:

- When the board will act on their nomination.

- When they will attend their first board meeting.

- Who will be in contact with them beforehand.

- Where they want to receive mail.

Leave them with a packet of information which will include such items as: board job description, bylaws, latest financial report and annual budget, board/committee roster, staff roster, annual report, minutes of last two board meetings and other pertinent information. See Figure 3.4, i.e., information packets.

9) The Honeymoon

Once the candidate has been elected, and has attended his or her first meeting, make sure they are supported. Have a fellow board member keep in touch with them for 6-12 months to: see how they are doing, answer questions, provide guidance and serve as a role model. See Figure 4.2 "Board Buddy" Guidelines. Be sure to provide the training and orientation needed to get the new volunteer up and running, feeling competent and effective. See Figure 4.3 for the Orientation Planning Outline.

10) What If They Say No?

Certainly you will extend invitations which are turned down. A prospect may already be actively involved on other community boards, job responsibilities may preclude joining your board, or other commitments may interfere. When this happens, several protocol steps are in order. **1)** make a friend, extend your organization's appreciation for the prospect's considerations and follow up with a letter of thanks: **2)** ask the prospect if you may approach them at a later date — they will usually be flattered: and **3)** keep in touch by sending your organization's newsletter, annual report and other information on a periodic or regular basis. Above all, leave a good impression behind.

FIGURE 3.5 ©*1996 C3 Publications*

49

SECTION 4

FROM "HELLO" TO "GOOD-BYE"

"If a board member gets little of what he or she wants from membership on the board, that member may seek a balance by reducing the time and effort they give to board work."

—*Robert D. Herman*

From the Welcome to ...

Orientation

Training

Support

CASE IN POINT ⇨

We all know of a Jeff. The person who agrees to accept a position on a local nonprofit board without really knowing much about the organization. Does this sound familiar? A quick pitch by a colleague at work, bland assent by Jeff, followed by a letter of welcome to the board and meeting notice two weeks later. But Jeff liked and trusted his friend, so he pushed his doubts aside and started attending board meetings.

Now, flash forward two years and ask Jeff how that board experience was for him.

"Well." He pauses and stares off in thought. "Good cause. Nice people."

"So overall it's been a good experience?"

Jeff smiles. "I didn't say that. In fact, it was mostly a waste."

"How so?"

"For one thing, the recruitment process was a joke. I know that now. I didn't then. I wasn't selected because of what I could bring to the organization—I was just the first person my friend Ralph saw.

"Frankly, I wasn't suited for that organization. Important cause, but I wouldn't have chosen it based on my personal passions and interests. And another thing, there wasn't any kind of orientation or training for new board members. I sat around like a lump for two years, trying to figure out what was going on, feeling guilty and ineffective. Gradually I began to get the picture. But what a waste of time. And then I learned one very important fact."

"What was that?"

"As a board member, after two years, I finally learned that I and my fellow board members were legally responsible for the organization: how it handled its money, how it dealt with employee issues, contracts, and so on. So there I was. Legally responsible for an organization I didn't understand all that well, and for which I had received absolutely no training or support."

"So what now?"

"I resigned. I'm not saying I didn't learn a lot. But it was seat-of-the pants, school of figure-it-out-for-yourself information. And I am not a fan of what I went through."

(Sound familiar?)

CARE & FEEDING

Here is how you can assure that Jeff's experience isn't visited on your new board members. Care and feeding isn't just a trite phrase. It is a real-time responsibility. Once the new slate has been elected to serve, it is important that they be given a responsible and enthusiastic welcome. The committee should consider this matter as carefully as any of its planning and deliberations thus far.

GETTING NEW BOARD MEMBERS OFF TO A GREAT START

The following are steps which may help get your new board members off to a great and sustainable beginning. See Figure 4.1 for full details about receiving new board members.

- Make confirming phone calls from Board Development Committee Chair, Board President and Chief Executive.

- Send letters of welcome from the Board President and Chief Executive.

- Assign each new board member a "board buddy." See Figure 4.2.

- Hold a reception, or other social event, for newly elected members to meet the other trustees, committee members, and staff.

- Assess your board meeting culture. Nothing speaks more forcefully about your organization than how those meetings are run.

- Provide thorough orientation for new board members. See Figure 4.3.

- Commit to ongoing board education.

- Initiate contact by the Chief Executive, show interest in helping the new board member get started. See Figure 4.4 for Board Member Information Form and Appendix F, "About My Board Service," page 85.

- Schedule follow-up contact by the Board Development Committee.

These steps will assure that new members become quickly involved and committed to your organization's mission. Adhering to well-planned steps will bring superior results. Candidates will feel valued, be impressed with your recruitment process, and the organization. And you will end up with people who are well suited to help carry your mission forward, and who will bring positive new energy into your organization for years to come.

Receiving the
New Board Member *Guidelines*

....

W e l c o m e

O r i e n t a t i o n

T r a i n i n g

Be prepared to receive new board members respectfully and professionally. Being asked to join an organization's governing body, after all, is an honor. Many who accept nomination do so in large measure because they are asked. They are responding to the honor of the invitation.

How will they feel about that honor when they meet your organizational reality—head on? Without thoughtful preparation and follow-through, that reality can often fall short of the honor. To avoid disappointment, and maximize the talent you have recruited, prepare diligently to welcome, orient and support your new board members.

AFTER ACCEPTANCE

Once an invitation to be nominated has been accepted, several steps of appreciation and welcome will help begin a thoughtful and thorough process of induction.

■ Phone Calls

The candidate should receive several brief, confirming telephone calls from the Chairperson of the Board Development Committee, Board President and the Chief Executive—in that order. *(No, three calls are not too many, just space them out.)*

— From The *Committee Chair*
Her/his call offers congratulations, provides verbal confirmation, responds to questions, tells candidate what will happen next, i.e., process, election, welcoming reception, first board meeting, assignment of "board buddy", etc.

— From The *Board President*
He/she calls to offer official appreciation for accepting nomination, asserts anticipation of meeting the person personally at the next board meeting, or special reception, where they will be introduced and meet the board, staff and board development committee members.

— From The *Chief Executive*
Telephone acknowledgment from the executive officer is a must: confirming details, answering any lingering questions, offering any additional information which candidate may request—and a warm welcome. See Figure 4.4, and Appendix F, page 85.

FIGURE 4.1 ©*1996 C3 Publications* 55

■ In Writing

Confirm each nomination in writing by the Chief Executive or Board Development Committee Chair, on behalf of the Board President and the board itself. The letter should verify next steps, i.e., his/her election to the board, a reception, first board meeting, orientation, and board contact person.

■ Personal Board Contact

Before candidates attend any meetings, receptions, et al, current board members are selected to be a point of contact; one for each new member. These "board buddies" are made known to the candidates and told how they may interact with them. An assigned "buddy" will make personal contact before the candidate's first board meeting or welcoming event, making sure new members feel wanted, valued and connected.

The "buddy" will sit with his/her assigned new member at board meetings, brief them about board procedure, and help them get up to speed on current board and organizational issues. Following the first few board meetings, each new member will be contacted by their board colleague to answer questions, get their initial impressions, and assure their comfort and understanding. This personal interaction will continue until the new member is effectively assimilated into the organization.

■ Social Event

A pleasant way to break the ice and help new board members feel-at-home is through a social event of some sort. Holding an after-work or pre-board meeting reception is a "low cost," "low fuss" way to do that. Provide light hors d'oeuvres and beverages, name badges, a pleasant room in which to mingle, and a strong attendance by the current board and senior staff. Have "board buddies" call the new board member invitees well ahead of time, get the date on their calendar, mail or fax directions to the site of the reception, and make sure their buddies are there to meet them. Then—enjoy. Such special treatment will be long remembered and appreciated.

■ Board Meetings

While every step mentioned is important in acclimating new board members—none is more critical than the board meetings themselves. The convened board can be the most powerful evidence of an effective organization—or reflect exactly the opposite.

Prior to electing new members to the board, it is useful to assess your "board meeting culture." More new board talent has been lost due to ineffectual board meetings than anything else. How often have you experienced "deadly" board culture? After all of your hard work of recruitment, new board members must see an effective board in action: timely meetings, important issues, action oriented agenda, energetic involvement of the members and wise use of the board members' time.

FIGURE 4.1 ©1996 C3 Publications

NOW IS A GOOD TIME TO ASSESS YOUR OWN BOARD CULTURE

- Are your board meetings energetic and alive? *(Board governance doesn't have to be dull.)*

- Are your meetings focused, with policy-setting and decision-making agendas?

- Are your meetings rampant with long, dull reports and rambling discussion over details best left to management, staff or committees?

- Are your board agendas tightly drawn and targeted to what actually has to happen? And are they lead in a crisp yet inclusive manner?

- Do you regularly include board education during meetings to enhance members' knowledge and capability? When board education is included, do you trim the regular agenda to absolute essentials?

- Can board members count on expeditious use of their time? Do your board meetings consistently run too long or are they usually brought in on a reasonably tight time line?

- Is an effort made to involve all board members in the meeting process? Is every member regularly given responsibilities to lead action item discussions or to give key reports, and are they regularly asked for their opinion and input? Or are your members mostly spectators?

- Are your board meetings fun? Do you acknowledge the importance of a positive social experience and allow time prior to meetings for members to enjoy one another? And do you encourage good humor during meetings on balance with conducting business in an effective manner?

- During your board meetings, do you regularly acknowledge or honor board members, other volunteers and staff, rewarding their special achievements or overall performance?

- In the end, will your new board members see efficiently run, energetic meetings with an involved membership getting business done while enjoying a positive social experience? If so, great! If not, do your homework before new members experience less than your best.

ORIENTING YOUR NEW BOARD MEMBERS

You owe every new board member a thorough orientation to your organization. Even if they have served on other boards, they should receive instruction regarding the specifics of your organization. Whether as an individual or as a group, make sure your new members understand the importance of an orientation and sense your commitment to that process.

Do not slide through this exercise. Involve key people: Board President, Chief Executive, senior staff, board officers and committee chairs. Be thorough, be upbeat (have fun), be intentional and be concise. Any useful orientation shouldn't run less than one or probably not more than three hours. It can be a tightly organized mini-seminar or more relaxed occasion with lunch included. A special evening event may also work well. It depends on the culture of your own organization. See Figure 4.3 for Orientation Planning Outline.

FIGURE 4.1 ©*1996 C3 Publications*

57

BOARD EDUCATION AND TRAINING

Once you have completed the orientation—don't forget ongoing education. Consider including several occasions for board training in your annual plan of work *(e.g., 2-4 times during the year)*. Often board members balk at another meeting. Be inventive, use scheduled board meetings, trim the usual agenda to bare bones essentials and incorporate a special training session. Be sure that the subjects are relevant and well presented. Using outside consultants or colleagues can help assure an attentive audience. Also, consider an annual board retreat, presented as part of any board's stewardship of service; meeting fiduciary and prudent service expectations.

SUBJECT FOR SUCH TRAINING WILL REFLECT YOUR ORGANIZATION'S SPECIFIC NEEDS

For example:

- leadership training,

- education on not-for-profit law,

- reviewing the role of the board,

- training on how a major gifts campaign is run,

- update on changes in your programs and services,

- briefings by experts in your field of endeavor,

- other subjects important to your organization.

The key is to "proactively schedule" board training. Board training could actually be part of the Board Development Committee's charge—to assure that the enhancement of board skills and knowledge is ongoing. With the Chief Executive and Board President, the committee can lead the planning and scheduling of board education sessions annually, championing the value and necessity of training with their board colleagues.

FIGURE 4.1 ©1996 C3 Publications

The "Board Buddy" *Guidelines*

Making the Connection

We mentioned the importance of a "board buddy" earlier. But additional emphasis is warranted. Newly elected board members may know very little about your organization. In spite of your best efforts to brief them, they will need help in *making the connection—* in translating all that has been thrown at them into an understanding of what is actually going on. This is where the "board buddy" comes in. But like every step along the way, matching your new board members with your experienced board colleagues should be handled with care. The following outline may help you with this task:

STEPS TO SELECTING THE PERSONAL BOARD CONTACT

■ After selecting a board candidate, choose a personal board contact for them as soon as possible to enhance the new member's assimilation into the organization.

■ Consider the match-up carefully. Choose a personal board contact versed in the affairs and history of the organization, knowledgeable of current board activities and who would enjoy being a mentor.

■ "Board buddy" match-ups might include: professional peers, similar age—or just the opposite, same geographic vicinity (i.e., riding to meetings together), those who might work on a committee together, and other factors you feel would make the relationship more effective.

DUTIES OF THE *"BOARD BUDDY"*

■ Immediately following, or just prior to, the election of the new board member, the assigned "board buddy" should call, introduce her/himself, extend congratulations, answer questions the person may have and discuss next steps: first board meeting, orientation, committee appointment.

■ That first board meeting is a "big deal" for a new board member. The board contact calls in advance, confirms attendance, goes over the agenda, assures that they will sit together and makes sure the new member is introduced to each board member one-on-one; informally if possible. After the board meeting, she/he calls to get the reaction of the new member, answers questions and offers assistance where needed.

■ Prior to the board orientation, contact the new member in advance to make sure the meeting is on their calendar and confirm arrangements to join them at the meeting.

■ The "board buddy" serves as a point of contact with the new member during their first year. Caution: *don't discontinue this contact too soon.* Obviously, over time the need for the initial close contact can, and should, be lessened. But remain alert to symptoms like: lack of attendance, non-participation at board meetings, and lack of follow-through on assignments. If these symptoms show up, look into ways to help the new member get back on track.

FIGURE 4.2 ©*1996 C3 Publications*

59

New Board Member
Orientation *Planning Outline*

LOGISTICS ✔

Possible orientation date/s: _____

Suggested location: _____

Preferred length of session: ☐ 3 hrs   ☐ 2 hrs   ☐ 1 hr   ☐ other: _____

Preferred time of day: ☐ morning ☐ noon ☐ afternoon ☐ evening

Proposed starting time: _____

Proposed ending time: _____

Will there be a break? ☐ Yes ☐ No

If yes, when? _____

MODEL ORIENTATION AGENDA

■ **Welcome, introductions:** *led by board president /other board officer/s.*

Name of person/s_____

■ **Overview of your organization:** *led by the CEO /other staff/ board member/s.*

Name of person/s_____

— Mission statement

— Brief history, past to present

— Organizational structure

■ **Programs and services:** *led by senior staff/committee chairs.*

Name of person/s_____

— Concise description of centerpiece programs / services

■ **Fiscal information:** *led by chair of finance committee/staff controller.*

Name of person/s_____

— Current budget, year-to-date

— General financial position

— Portfolio *(if relevant)*

FIGURE 4.3 ©*1996 C3 Publications*

■ **Financial Development:** *led by volunteer chair/development director.*

Name of person/s_____

— Organization revenue sources

— Current major funding activities and plans

— Board role in development

■ **Strategic Plans:** *led by board president/CEO/other board officer/member.*

Name of person/s_____

— Status of planning process

— Future vision

— Discussion of important issues facing your organization, challenges, future opportunities, special concerns, etc.

■ **Board Governance:** *led by board president/other board officer.*

Name of person/s_____

— Board process defined

— Board role and responsibilities

■ **Distribution of Board Materials:** *give new members information previously withheld.*

Name of person/s_____

— Board manual

— Strategic plan

— Updated calendar of future meetings

■ **Conclusion of Session:** *Board President and Chief Executive wrap up meeting with thanks, information about next board meeting or other functions/duties—and an invitation to tour the offices and facilities. Meet staff—the real faces—and see centers of activity.*

Name of person/s_____

■ **Tour of Facilities:** *led by CEO and/or senior staff.*

FIGURE 4.3 ©1996 C3 Publications

Board Member
Information and Operations *Form*

Please complete this form and return to the Chief Executive Officer at your earliest convenience. The information you provide will aid in facilitating your service on the Board of Directors. Thank you.

Please type or print

COMMUNICATION AND CONTACT INFORMATION

Date: _____

Name: _____

Note: If you have a *"nickname"* you prefer to be called, e.g., *"Bill"* instead of William, please indicate so here:

Nickname: _____

Where do you prefer receiving our organization's mail? ☐ Work ☐ Home

Name of your organization: _____

Your Title: _____

Street Address: _____

Mailing Address: _____

_____
   (City)   (State)   (Zip)

Name of Admin. Asst. / other contact person: _____

This person's direct phone number (if any): _____

Home Address: _____

_____
   (City)   (State)   (Zip)

Day Phone: _____ Evening Phone: _____

Fax : _____ Mobile Phone : _____ E-mail: _____

Name of Spouse / Significant other: _____

BOARD SERVICE INFORMATION

Date you joined our board: _____ (*Month*) _____ (*Year*)

Who recruited you to join our board? _____

Who is your personal board contact (*board buddy*)? _____

What most influenced your decision to join our Board of Directors?
(*check all that apply*) ✔

☐ Our mission   ☐ The person who asked you

☐ Organization's reputation   ☐ Wanted to serve the community

☐ A specific program or service: _____

Which program/service? _____

Other reason/s: _____

As of this date, have you completed an organizational orientation? ☐ Yes ☐ No

Have you accepted a position on one of our working committees? ☐ Yes ☐ No

If yes, which committee? _____

If no, is there a specific area of organizational service you are interested in?

☐ Yes. Area of interest: _____

☐ Not yet. I'll need more information before deciding where I'd like to serve.

Have you previously served on community not-for-profit boards? ☐ Yes ☐ No

If yes, please list the most representative examples of your previous board service.

_____

_____

Other: Memberships and Associations (professional societies, civic organizations, social affiliations, business organizations, etc.).

_____

_____

ADDITIONAL INFORMATION REQUESTS: (*Please indicate the availability of the following*)

☐ I am enclosing my resume or bio sheet for organizational information and use.

☐ I am enclosing a "mug" photo (*b/w, glossy, 5"x7" or 8"x10"*).

☐ I understand that the information I am providing is to be used only by the organization, i.e., announcing my board appointment, and for other pertinent purposes to enhance our work.

FIGURE 4.4 ©*1996 C3 Publications*   *63*

OTHER MATTERS: *(Additional information to be given or requests to be made.)*

_____

_____

_____

_____

_____

_____

_____

_____

_____

_____

_____

Signed: _____ Date: _____

The Exit Interview

....

Saying Good - bye

CASE IN POINT ⇨

Marge had been a board member of the Environmental Council for six years. Prior to that, she had been a grass roots volunteer for a number of years. She was invested.

Six months ago she reached the maximum number of consecutive years which she could serve on the board. Even though she understood the need for term limits, Marge was nevertheless disappointed that she would no longer be an active board member. And she was still feeling a sense of loss months later. Oh, there were some very nice words spoken at her last board meeting—and she did have the plaque and all.

But that was it. She had some very deep feelings for the cause and commitment to the organization. And now that was all gone. There had been no offer to continue in some other capacity as a volunteer. No phone call from the Chief Executive—a man she had known for over a decade.

And on top of that, she would have liked a chance to share some concerns she had and to encourage the organization to continue along a certain path. One day she was part of something important to her, the next—nothing.

(How should Marge have been treated?)

As you are welcoming your newest board members, you may also be saying good-bye to some old friends. Lest you overlook the Marge's on your board, let's consider the protocol—and the opportunity—of engaging with departing board members.

RECOGNITION

To begin with, you may want to arrange occasions of recognition and appreciation. Always remember that retiring board members will continue to be among your most avid supporters and advocates in the community *(or they should be)*. Demonstrations of appreciation also show incoming board members that their role within your organization will be respected.

EXIT INTERVIEW

After the awards and recognition, you have a wonderful opportunity to ask outgoing board members for a status report. Use exit interviews to gain valuable feedback from people who have been a part of your organization for some time. The interview is not only a courtesy, it is quite frankly an important window from which to gain valuable feedback.

DOING IT RIGHT

The "exiting" process should not be cursory. Approach this opportunity with dignity and warmth. Get on the retiring board member's calendar. Let her/him know the purpose of the meeting and then come prepared. Decide who should best attend the meeting, i.e., the Chief Executive, the Board President, or both; perhaps a longtime board colleague would be a good choice. Use whichever approach is likely to gain the most valuable feedback. A written report of each visit will help assure that appropriate action is considered based on what is learned. A letter of appreciation is sent afterward from the most suitable party, and, if desirable, an invitation to remain involved in some non-board capacity. See Figure 4.5 for Exit Interview Form.

The Exit Interview *Form*

....

Suggested Exit

Interview Inquiries

■ Tell me (us) how you first came to be involved with our organization.

Notes: _____

_____

_____

■ What have been your most meaningful areas of service? Are there specific volunteer projects, board activity or organizational actions that stand out?

Notes: _____

_____

_____

■ Have there been organizational events or issues that were disappointing? If so, how can we prevent such occurrences in the future and improve our capabilities in those areas?

Notes: _____

_____

_____

■ What do you view as our organization's greatest strengths; our major assets?

Notes: _____

_____

_____

■ Conversely, where do we need to improve; what are our primary weaknesses?

Notes: _____

_____

_____

FIGURE 4.5 ©*1996 C3 Publications*   67

■ Looking ahead, what advice would you give your colleagues on the board about guiding the organization toward a successful future?

Notes: _____

_____

_____

Note: *Allow time for the exiting board member to discuss other issues which they may want to share, expound on or get off their chest. Also, if desirable, this may be a good time to ask this person if they would be interested in continuing their involvement in some non-board capacity.*

FIGURE 4.5 ©1996 C3 Publications

Sustaining Leadership

....

"Don't Quit !"

The final step of the board development process is, as the fitness coach says, "Don't Quit!" After those welcoming handshakes, congratulatory slaps on the back among your committee colleagues, and sighs of relief that your goal was accomplished, don't rest on your laurels. Board competency requires continual diligence. So before your committee goes on hiatus, take the time to assure that board development will indeed go on; will be sustained and constant.

HERE ARE SEVERAL HOUSEKEEPING STEPS TO CONSIDER

■ **Evaluate The Recruitment Process Just Completed**
What worked? What didn't? What needs changing and what should be retained? Has the committee made a formal report of its activities to the board? If not, when should such a report be scheduled to keep the board informed and engaged? See Figure 4.6 for Board Development Evaluation Form.

■ **Revisit Your Board Development Plan**
Does it still seem on target? Do you need to modify your goals, or other elements of the plan? Who will create a draft of a revised plan? By what time should a revised plan be completed?

■ **What Is The Status Of Your Board Development Committee?**
Are some members at the end of their term *(usually one year)?* How many members want to stay on the committee? Which members should be asked to accept another term? Who will chair the committee during the next term—a current committee member or another board member? Will there be a base of experience among remaining members? If the committee will go through a major transformation, who on the organization's board should be considered for membership?

■ **Is The Original Time Line Still Viable?**
Do you need to move to the next phase of your board development plan as scheduled, or should the dates be changed? What would a revised schedule look like?

■ **Don't Overlook Support Of New Board Members**
Have your new members received their formal orientation? Does each new board member have a "board buddy"? Have you polled your new members to see how they felt about your recruitment process? Has additional board training been scheduled?

■ **Plan For Continuity**
As stewards of board competency, how will you maintain an ongoing process of board development? What are your next steps?

Board Development
Evaluation *F o r m*

At the conclusion of a board development cycle, it will be helpful for the Board Development Committee to evaluate how the process worked. Have each member complete the following form and then compare and combine results to identify changes or improvements to be undertaken in the future.

HOW DID WE DO?

Rate the steps in our board development process as follows:

1 = Very Well Done
2 = Well Done
3 = Moderately Well Done
4 = Fair
5 = Poor

■ Status and readiness:

_____ Board charge _____ Forming committee _____ Audit _____ Assessment

■ Preparation stage:

_____ Creating development plan _____ Attention to process

■ Recruitment action:

_____ Identifying candidates _____ Qualifying candidates _____ Setting slate

_____ Setting the approach _____ Creating the message

_____ Getting to the ask _____ Success in securing desired candidates

■ Support of new board members:

_____ The welcome process _____ Assigning board buddy _____ Election

_____ First board meeting _____ Orientation _____ Follow-up

_____ Plans for ongoing board education

■ Retiring board members:

_____ Formal recognition and appreciation for service rendered

_____ Scheduling and conducting exit interviews

FIGURE 4.6 ©*1996 C3 Publications*

OVERALL, HOW DID WE DO?

_____

_____

_____

_____

_____

_____

_____

_____

THE BOARD DEVELOPMENT PLAN ✔

- ■ Did our plan work? ☐ Yes ☐ Mostly ☐ Mostly Not ☐ No

- ■ What would you change about our plan?

_____

_____

_____

BOARD DEVELOPMENT COMMITTEE ✔

- ■ Did committee make-up provide necessary skills, contacts and access?

  ☐ Yes ☐ Mostly ☐ Mostly Not ☐ No

- ■ If you were to suggest additional members, what attributes would they have?

_____

_____

_____

BOARD DEVELOPMENT TIME LINE ✔

- ■ Was our original planned time line viable?

  ☐ Yes ☐ Mostly ☐ Mostly Not ☐ No

- ■ If you feel we should change our time line, what would you do differently?

_____

_____

_____

FIGURE 4.6 ©*1996 C3 Publications*

71

REPORTING TO THE BOARD ✔

■ Was the committee diligent in advising the board of its activities?

☐ Yes ☐ Mostly ☐ Mostly Not ☐ No

■ Comments:

_____

_____

_____

ONGOING BOARD EDUCATION ✔

■ Did the committee consider its opportunity to facilitate board education?

☐ It was considered, but declined by committee.

☐ Not considered.

☐ Committee will investigate the option further.

☐ Committee will plan future board education.

☐ Board education will be staff driven with committee input.

CHANGED OR RETAINED?

■ What about our board development process should be changed?

_____

_____

_____

■ What about our board development process should be retained?

_____

_____

_____

FIGURE 4.6 ©1996 C3 Publications

Some Closing Thoughts

....

" H a v e   F u n !   "

In the final analysis, life is supposed to be fun! And as important as is your task of developing and sustaining leadership, it is good to keep a sense of humor about ourselves as well.

As I poked around looking for something on the lighter side about the role of leadership, I ran across *The Cynic's Lexicon,* a collection by Jonathan Green. Green, an Oxford educated journalist, describes his lexicon as "an unashamed collection of amoral advice." A perfect reference to help us address the seriousness of our task with a smile on our faces.

So I looked up "leadership" in among the cynicisms and ran across a couple of quotes to help us keep our sense of humor and perspective:

"A revolution requires of its leaders a record of infallibility. If they do not possess it they are expected to invent it." —Murray Kempton

"A leader is a man who has the ability to get other people to do what they don't want to do and like it." —Harry S. Truman

While we might not subscribe to the cynicism of Mr. Kempton or President Truman, I'm sure they would agree that true, voluntary leadership is neither infallible nor can it be sustained through manipulation.

Nor does true leadership spring forth with no nurturing, nor standards of excellence, nor expectation of achievement. It comes from commitment like yours; commitment to bringing together the right human talent, matching it with the right challenges and opportunities and then providing support so those talents can successfully serve your mission.

So, congratulations! I commend your efforts. Your organization, and its mission, will be the beneficiary —and so will you.

George B. Wright

P.S. If you have questions or comments about this book, wish to discuss your board development process, or to learn about the services of **C3 Strategies**, please contact me.

Call: **(503) 223-0268**

Write: **C3 Strategies**
3495 NW Thurman Street
Portland, OR 97210

APPENDIX

"I do believe private institutions, where citizen volunteers work for the common or general good, form a fundamental part of the fabric of American life."

—*Robert Wood*

Board
Profile *G R I D*

EXPERIENCE / SKILLS	Mary Smith									TOTAL
Accounting										
Banking										
Business / Corporate										
Education										
Employee Relations										
Fund Development										
Government										
Health / Medicine										
Investments										
Law										
Marketing / Public Relations										
Nonprofit Management										
CONNECTIONS / INFLUENCE										
Civic Groups										
Corporate Community										
Ethnic / Cultural Groups										
Government										
Media										
Nonprofit Agencies										
Neighborhood Associations										
DEMOGRAPHICS										
Female										
Male										
Ethnic / Cultural Minority:										
— Asian										
— African American										
— Caucasian										
— Hispanic / Latino										
— Native American										
— Other:										
Under 35 years										
From 35 – 50 years										
From 51 – 65 years										
Over 65 years										

Board Profile *G R I D*
(Continued)

GEOGRAPHY										TOTAL
City										
Suburbs										
County										
State										
Regional										
National										
International										
Other:										
BOARD / COMMITTEE EXPERIENCE										
Less than 1 year										
1 - 5 years										
6 - 9 years										
10+ years										
Executive Committee										
Fund Development Committee										
Board Development Committee										
Program Committee										
Planning Committee										
Other:										
OTHER										

Essential Duties & Responsibilities for Effective Boards

1. Define the organization's mission, commit to its intended outcome—then constantly revisit that mission, re-defining and revising as needed.

2. Select the chief executive, set clear expectations, provide full support and regularly review his or her performance.

3. Assure that the organization regularly engages in effective, visioning and planning and that the board fully supports and participates in that process.

4. Assure adequate resources through significant personal contributions of each board member, support of and participation in financial development planning and implementation, and stewardship of all resources.

5. Conduct an annual assessment of its own performance.

6. Operate with credibility, be free of conflicts of interest and recognize the responsibility to serve as ambassadors, advocates and stewards of the organization within the community.

7. Assure that the directors meet their responsibility to attend and participate in board meetings, lending the full scope of their individual skills and expertise for positive outcome.

8. Assure capable future board leadership by supporting and participating in an ongoing program of board development and recruitment.

9. Serve as court of resolution for problematic issues which fall outside the purview of management, handling all such matters with the highest ethical standards.

10. Recognize board directorship as a state of temporary stewardship.

The Duties & Responsibilities of the Board in its Relationship with the CEO

1. Before hiring its executive director, the not-for-profit board of directors should look to itself. Is the organization prepared to bring in a new director? Has the board assessed its own performance as part of inviting candidates to consider the organization's top professional position? Has the board revisited its mission and its vision of the future? If not, that process should be completed. Only then is the organization ready to share its expectations and opportunities with potential CEOs.

2. The hiring process should be thoughtful and professional. The board is hiring the person who will not only manage the affairs of the organization, but who will partner with them to create the vision and strategies to carry the organization toward fulfillment of its mission. When the task of selecting a CEO is thrust upon them, it is the single most important job board directors will ever have with that organization. Immediate and long-term success may depend on the selection.

3. Setting expectations for the CEO is an obligation of the board. It is dereliction on the one hand, and unfair on the other, for a board to expect its director to function without clear standards of expectation—both general operating policies and mission and vision expectations . This also requires the board to plan, to know where it wants to go and for what purpose. Expectations then provide the basis for assessing performance.

4. Supporting the CEO is an absolute necessity for prudent board stewardship. The board must provide the director with clear direction, supporting him or her fully in pursuit of the organization's goals. This requires a board to remain faithful to its governance role, and not enter into micro management. Board directors should live up to their responsibilities and agreements at all levels, including respect for the management role of the CEO and providing him or her the room and moral support to do the job.

5. CEO performance evaluations are often poorly implemented by not-for-profit boards, or are not done at all. The board has an obligation as the governing body to assess the performance of its chief executive. It is unfair to the organization and the director to leave this responsibility undone. Assessment of professional performance is a positive act. It provides the CEO vital feedback on how his or her work is perceived. It provides a forum for discussion—to acknowledge and reinforce the positive and to identify areas where change or improvement may be needed. Most importantly, it validates the partnership between the board and the CEO. True, the board does the hiring and firing, but everything in between is based on trust and mutual expectations. The CEO should expect and receive a thorough, thoughtful evaluation.

6. Board self-assessment is equally important. No board should conduct an evaluation of its chief executive without the honesty of assessing its own performance. The two are inextricably linked. How can a board effectively evaluate its CEO if it hasn't asked itself, "How did we do in meeting our obligations?" Board self-assessment should be as honest and thorough as that of the CEO.

7. If problems arise between the board and the CEO, they should be handled with total honesty and the highest ethical standards. Once problems are identified, the board president must lead quick and thoughtful resolution. There must be no secrecy beyond initial confidentiality of disclosure. Under no circumstances should the board hold meetings without the knowledge of the CEO. Nor should individual board members engage in private meetings with any staff regarding CEO performance. Once a problem is identified, the board president should fully inform the CEO and arrange to bring the appropriate parties together for positive dialogue and look for effective resolution. The board should remember its obligation to support its chief executive to the fullest extent possible. All decisions regarding the future of the CEO should be based on thoughtful execution of the highest ethical standards.

8. The strength of the Board/CEO partnership, then, comes from commitment to a process of planning, setting of realistic expectations, regular performance evaluations of the CEO and the Board and ethical resolution of problems.

M O D E L   D O C U M E N T

Board Of Directors Job Description

I, _____ , recognizing the important responsibility I am undertaking in serving as a member of the Board of Directors of _____ , hereby personally pledge to carry out in a trustworthy and diligent manner all duties and obligations inherent in my role as a Director.

MY ROLE:

I acknowledge that my primary role as a member of the Board of Directors is to contribute to the development of the _____ 's mission and to participate in governing the implementation of that mission.

My secondary role is to fulfill the functions of office set forth in the organization's bylaws and described in the job descriptions incorporated into the Board of Director's Policy Manual. The implementation of this role is expressly limited to those activities and functions not directly or indirectly delegated to staff, committees and task forces.

I understand that I have a fiduciary responsibility to the organization and that it is my duty to approve all budgets and programs of work.

(**OPTIONAL:** Further, I understand that so long as I carry out my duties and responsibilities in good faith and to the best of my ability, I will generally be free from any liability for the debts and actions of the organization as provided in *(cite local/state statutes which may be applicable).*

MY DUTIES:

I pledge to willingly use my best efforts to carry out the following duties as a Director with integrity, due care and enthusiasm:

1. To attend all meetings of the Board as scheduled, which includes (monthly, quarterly, annual, etc.) meetings, and any special (i.e., board retreat, planning) or emergency meetings as may be required.

2. To actively participate and attend meetings of committees or task forces on which I serve. I understand that I will be asked to serve on at least one committee and/or hold one leadership position.

3. To come prepared to contribute to the discussion of issues and business to be addressed at scheduled meetings, having read the agenda and all background support material relevant to the meeting.

4. To observe the parliamentary procedures outlined in Robert's Rules of Order, or Sturgis' Standard Code of Parliamentary Procedure, and manifest collegial conduct in all meetings I attend.

5. To willingly support the organization financially with what is a substantial contribution for me. I understand that no quotas have been set and that no standards of measurement have been formed.

6. To actively participate in fund raising activities of the organization; e.g., personal solicitation / major gift campaigns, special events, etc.

7. To assist and support cultivation activities of new or existing corporate, foundation, individual and planned gift donors or prospects.

8. To avoid conflicts of interest between my position as a Board member and my personal and professional life as outlined in the organization's Conflict of Interest Statement. If such a conflict does arise, I will declare that conflict before the Board, will refrain from participating in the discussion and will refrain from voting on any matters in which I have such a conflict of interest.

9. To maintain strict confidentiality of all business conducted in executive session.

10. To thoughtfully review all actions taken by the Board and vote for what I believe. If in a minority position on an issue, I will express my opinion prior to voting. After the vote, so long as my conscience dictates, I will support all actions taken by the Board in a positive manner.

11. To agree to chair or serve on committees and task forces to which I am appointed, attend their meetings and participate in the accomplishment of their objectives. If I chair a committee or task force, I agree to: (a) hold its meetings on a regularly scheduled basis until all objectives are accomplished; (b) ensure that agendas and support materials are mailed to all members in advance of meetings; (c) refrain from implementing strategies or taking actions that have not been reviewed and approved by the Board of Directors or expressly delegated for action to the committee or task force within Board prescribed guidelines; (d) conduct meetings in an orderly, fair and efficient manner; and (e) make progress reports as requested by the Board of Directors.

12. I acknowledge that my responsibility as a Director is to deal with policy issues and to support the professional staff in their decisions regarding administration and management.

13. To represent the organization in a positive and professional manner at all times and in all places.

If, for any reason, I find myself unable to carry out the above duties as best I can, or am unable to attend 75% of the scheduled board meetings, I agree to discuss with the President of the Board or Board Development Committee my future obligations in serving on the Board of Directors.

Dated: _____

Signature:_____

THE MOTIVES AND INCENTIVES OF VOLUNTEER INVOLVEMENT

When seeking leadership for boards of directors, or other volunteer posts, it is important to understand what motivates people. And further, what are the incentives which will activate those motives? For instance, studies have considered why very busy professionals add volunteer work to their already demanding lives. The answer is diverse and tied to an interesting mix of motives and incentives. Matching the motives of career professionals with the incentives offered by the voluntary organization can affect the performance of these volunteers, as well as their attitude.

TYPES OF MOTIVES AND INCENTIVES

For the purposes of this discussion, there are three types of motives. "Motives refer to predispositions to act when conditions are favorable, or can be made more favorable, to the attainment of goals valued by the individual" (Knoke & Wright-Isak, 1982).

- **Altruistic Motives:** These are based on feelings of a strong desire and selfless concern to help others. These volunteers usually have no regard for personal gain.

   Altruistic Incentives: Organizational incentives for the altruistic volunteer center around knowing they are serving a good cause.

- **Self-Interest Motives:** In this case, a person motivated by self-interest may serve as a volunteer to advance his or her professional career, because it is expected by an employer, or to receive other personal benefits, i.e., training, contacts, etc.

   Self-Interest Incentives: These incentives are tangible, measurable rewards, such as skills acquired in a voluntary position or status achieved, both of which could help career advancement, or meet other personal goals.

- **Social Motives:** When socially motivated, volunteers have a strong desire to identify with a group and to form social bonds with others.

   Social Incentives: Incentives center around social activities, formal ceremonies and events where interaction with people is the focus.

Recruiting volunteers is a never-ending responsibility for every voluntary organization. It is a process fraught with the incessant quest for strong volunteer leadership, the complexity of matching people to task and the competition within the not-for-profit sector for leadership.

Certainly, volunteers do not fall cleanly and precisely into these three classifications; and there are ramifications well beyond the mere definitions given here. However, it will serve an organization's leadership development objectives to consider the role of motives and incentives when recruiting volunteers.

ABOUT MY BOARD SERVICE

....

Personal Reflections
& Expectations

As a new member of our Board of Directors, you may find it helpful to reflect on your personal reasons, expectations and goals for agreeing to serve. Feel free to share this information with our Chief Executive or retain for your own personal records. The goal is to enhance your experience as a Board member.

1. I became a Board member for the following reasons: (e.g., learn new skills, gain new contacts, give back to the community)

   _____

   _____

2. I have the following abilities and qualities to offer the Board:

   _____

   _____

3. I am willing to contribute to the Board and organizational process by:

   _____

   _____

4. In order to be an effective Board member, I need to know:

   _____

   _____

5. From other Board members and staff, I expect:

   _____

   _____

6. At the end of my term, I would feel a sense of pride and fulfillment if we on the Board had:

   _____

   _____

   _____

Name *(optional)*:_____

About The Author

George B. Wright served for over 26 years as a professional in the not-for-profit sector. He managed at every key staff position within 501(c)(3) not-for-profit organizations, including the CEO level. In 1991, he and his wife, Betsy, both left administrative posts in not-for-profit organizations; he as Executive Director of the American Lung Association of Oregon, she as Executive Director of Ronald McDonald House in Portland. Together they formed C3 Strategies, a consulting company serving not-for-profit clients, located in Portland, Oregon.

Subsequent to founding C3 Strategies, Mr. Wright engaged in his lifelong love — writing. Within a year he had written **The Not-For-Profit CEO, A Survivor's Manual,** now in its third printing, and launched C3 Publications as an adjunct to their consulting practice. In 1993, the author began publishing a national subscription newsletter, **The NFP-CEO Monthly Letter,** which has member subscribers across the country.

As a partner in C3 Strategies, Mr. Wright focuses on improving not-for-profit organizational performance through board development, management support and organizational assessment. It was through his hands-on work with clients, and his long professional passion for enhancing boards, that he was moved to create this manual: **Beyond Nominating.** Other services of C3 Strategies include: strategic and fund development planning, capital campaigns and major gifts.

How to order more copies of this book . . . and other resources from C3 Publications

BEYOND NOMINATING —*A Guide to Gaining and Sustaining Successful Not-For-Profit Boards*
A road map to attracting the competent, talented and visionary volunteer leadership every not-for-profit organization wants and needs. Here are the tools to help you: assess, plan, and effectively recruit the best board leadership. You will want to order enough copies of this manual so that each of your board development committee members can have their own, personal copy. Beginning with as few as 6 copies, you are eligible for a quantity discount. ISBN 0-9632655-1-2, $25.00 each, paperback. By George B. Wright.

THE NOT-FOR-PROFIT CEO, A SURVIVOR'S MANUAL *(Third Printing!)*
Before you recruit another board member, raise another dollar or prepare your next budget, read this book. In today's environment of increasing scrutiny and competition, it's critical to apply the author's six management checkpoints (✔): 1) Managing a Democracy, 2) Search & Deploy, 3) Relate, Relate, Facilitate, 4) Dollars In, Dollars Out, 5) Out and About, and 6) the Wide Angle Lens. A valuable refresher for veteran NFP CEOs, a guidebook for the new CEO and a view through the looking glass for future CEOs. ISBN 0-9632655-0-4, $11.95 each, paperback. By George B. Wright.

THE NOT-FOR-PROFIT CEO MONTHLY LETTER
The focus of this publication is the practicing NFP CEO. Each month receive 8 full pages addressing issues critical to the job of managing the not-for-profit organization. Issues like: leadership, change in the third sector, competing for funds, managing boards, dealing with stress, the latest from the IRS, and experts on technical matters like: human resources, marketing, and audits. The Monthly Letter is edited by a former NFP CEO with over 26 years in the NFP sector. (Sample issue sent on request).
Published monthly, eight pages 8 1/2 X 11, annual subscription $89, 12 issues. George B. Wright, Editor.

- ✄

ORDER *FORM*

Quantity

_____ **Beyond Nominating** $25

_____ **The Not-For-Profit CEO**
A Survivor's Manual $11.95

☐ YES! I want a 1-year subscription to:
The Not-For-Profit CEO Monthly Letter
12 Issues / $89 – Includes shipping/handling
☐ Please Send Sample Issue

Total Amount of Order $ _____

Applicable Book Discount $ _____

SUBTOTAL $ _____

Add Shipping / Handling $ _____

TOTAL PAYMENT ENCLOSED $ _____

☐ Check / Money Order
   Make checks payable to C3 Publications

☐ VISA   ☐ Mastercard   **VISA**   **MasterCard**

Card # _____

Exp. Date _____

Signature _____

Name _____

Organization _____

Address _____

City _____ State _____ Zip _____

Daytime Phone (____) _____

Mail or fax your order to:

C3 Publications
3495 NW Thurman Street   *(503) 223-0268*
Portland, Oregon 97210   *Fax (503) 223-3083*

Note: Discounts are for multiple copies of the same book title only.

Discount Schedule (books only)	Shipping & Handling	
Qty. Ordered	**Order Size**	**S & H**
	Up to $12+	$2.50
1-5 . . . . 0%	$13 – 25+	$4.50
6-9 . . . . 5%	$26 – 40+	$5.75
10-24 . . . . 10%	$41 – 50+	$7.00
25-49 . . . . 20%	$51 – 75+	$9.00
50-99 . . . . 30%	$76 – 150+	$10.00
100+ 40%	$151 – 250+	$12.50
	$251 +	5% of Order